VISION BOARD
CLIP ART BOOK *for Women*

500+ Inspiring Images, Quotes & Affirmations to Manifest Your Dream Life

MELANIE FRENCH

Copyright © 2025 by Melanie French
All rights reserved.

No part of this publication, *Vision Board Clip Art Book for Women: 500+ Inspiring Images, Quotes & Affirmations to Manifest Your Dream Life*, may be reproduced, stored in a retrieval system, or transmitted in any form or by any means—electronic, mechanical, photocopying, recording, or otherwise—without the prior written permission of the author, except in the case of brief quotations used in reviews or articles.

This book is lovingly dedicated to all women who believe in the power of their vision and are brave enough to turn dreams into reality.

**You don't just dream.
You control your reality.**

YOUR
VISION BOARD
A TOOL FOR TRANSFORMATION

Imagine waking up every morning knowing that your dreams are no longer wishes but your reality. You've built a career you love, explored breathtaking destinations, created meaningful relationships, and achieved financial freedom.
How does it feel? What does it look like?

Visualization is not just a fantasy — it's a powerful method for turning your desires into tangible success. A Vision Board helps you not only dream but act.
Remember, you don't need to wait for a new year, a Monday, or the perfect moment to begin. Dreaming is timeless, and your journey begins the moment you decide to take action.

This book is your guide to crafting the perfect Vision Board. Inside, you'll find an inspiring collection of images, motivational quotes, and practical tips to help you manifest your goals in every area of your life.

Color Coding Your Dreams

Understanding the Energy Behind Each Section
Before you dive into crafting your Vision Board, let's talk about color.
Each area of your life holds a unique energy, and color helps to activate it.
In traditional vision boards, especially those inspired by Feng Shui, every section is more than just a square. It's a focused space of intention and energy.
This method is based on the Bagua Map, an ancient Feng Shui tool that divides your space into nine life areas: wealth, fame, love, health, family, creativity, knowledge, career, and travel.
Each zone has a corresponding color, direction, and purpose. When used mindfully, these elements can gently influence your mindset and bring more harmony and momentum into your life.
Use this page as your compass. Align your goals with powerful visual energy. Let each color carry a purpose. Let each image tell a story.

PAINT YOUR LIFE IN EVERY COLOR!

Don't just build a board — design a destiny that's bold, vibrant, and full of magic.
The layout and structure of this book follow a mindful system inspired by balance, vision, and timeless wisdom.

LET THE COLORS LEAD THE WAY — AND LET YOUR VISION SHINE.

- FINANCES
- FAME & RECOGNITION
- LOVE & ROMANCE
- FAMILY & ROOTS
- HEALTH & VITALITY
- CREATIVITY & CHILDREN
- KNOWLEDGE & GROWTH
- CAREER & WORK
- TRAVEL & ADVENTURE

"Success is her mindset.
Wealth is her result.

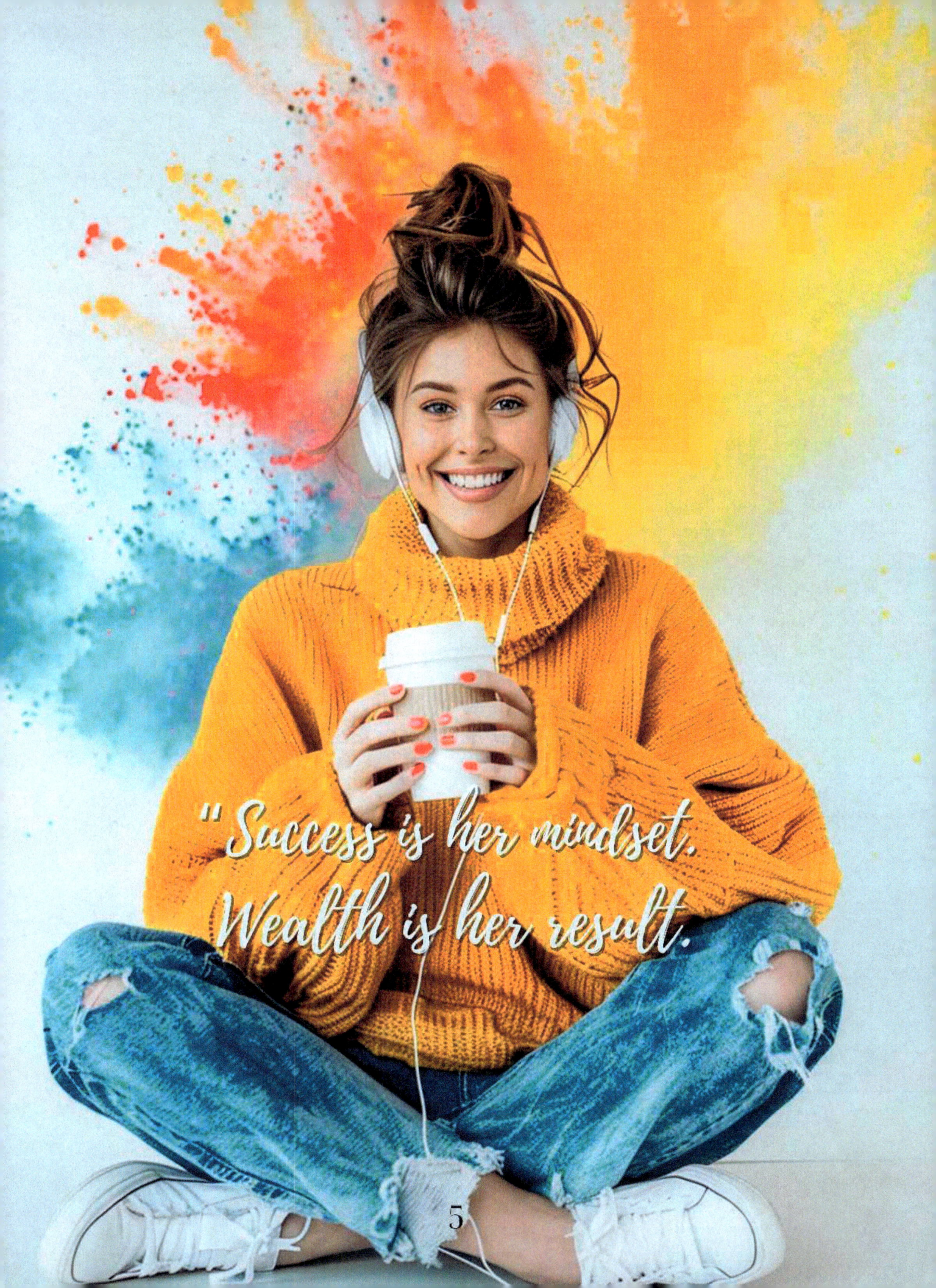

HOW TO MAKE A VISION BOARD — A GENTLE GUIDE JUST FOR YOU

Start with YOU

Choose a fresh, smiling photo of yourself — one where you truly feel beautiful and radiant. Your Vision Board begins with you, the leading lady of your own story. Don't be shy — let the photo reflect your joy, confidence, and light.

Define the Areas of Your Life

Break your dreams down into 9 life areas:
 – Career, Money, Love, Health, Family, Travel, Knowledge, Creativity, Fame & Recognition

You can follow the Feng Shui-inspired color-coded grid (Bagua Map) or simply organize them in a way that feels right to you.

Gather Your Dream Images

Look for visuals that spark joy or give you a powerful "yes!" feeling:
 – Places you want to travel to
 – Dream home or kitchen
 – Scenes from movies that reflect your ideal life
 – A happy couple embracing
 – Inspiring quotes
 – Money, contracts, or symbols of success

📌 *If it makes you smile, it belongs on your board.*

Arrange Your Board with Intention

You can follow a structured layout based on the 9 sections —
 Or simply follow your intuition.
There's no right or wrong — the only rule is to fill it with energy and meaning.

Add Words & Affirmations

Include empowering words or short phrases, like:
 – "I'm living my dream life."
 – "I travel, love, create, and thrive."
Feel free to mix fonts, stickers, colors — anything that feels fun and personal.

Place Your Vision Board Where You'll See It Daily

Keep your board somewhere visible — a place where it can quietly inspire you every day.
It's not a secret file — it's your map to the life you're building.

And remember: you don't need to know how everything will happen.

Visualize first — the action will follow.

HEALTH & VITALITY
STRONG MIND. STRONG BODY. RADIANT LIFE.

WHEALTH

VISUALIZE YOUR HEALTH GOALS

Motivational Quote
"My body is my home. I nourish it with love, strength, and intention."

How to Use This Section
Visualize Your Health Goals:
What does vitality mean to you? Is it boundless energy, a calm mind, glowing skin, or peaceful sleep?
Select images that reflect your healthiest self — nature walks, fresh meals, yoga, and moments of true rest.

Affirm Your Wellness:
Add phrases like:
– "I choose foods that energize and heal me."
– "My mind is clear. My body is powerful."
– "Every cell in my body radiates health."
– "I am in love with how I feel."

Set Intentions for Wellness:
Define what balance looks like:
– Nourishing meals
– Gentle movement
– Rest & hydration
– Saying "yes" to joy and "no" to burnout

Visualization Practice: Embodying Vitality
Take a few quiet minutes each morning:
– Close your eyes
– Picture yourself full of energy, moving freely, smiling, radiant
– Imagine every cell in your body glowing with health
– Feel gratitude for your body's wisdom and strength
Repeat: "This is how I choose to feel."

Inspiring Images to Include
- *Yoga, stretching, and nature movement*
- *Colorful smoothie bowls and herbal tea*
- *Serene sleep spaces and sunlit rooms*
- *Crystals, oils, breathwork symbols*
- *Water, sunlight, hands on the heart*
- *Journals, rituals, peaceful morning light*

Healthy Habits to Manifest
– Stretch your body with gratitude
– Eat for energy, not emotion
– Let rest be sacred
– Move daily — even gently
– Celebrate your body for all it does

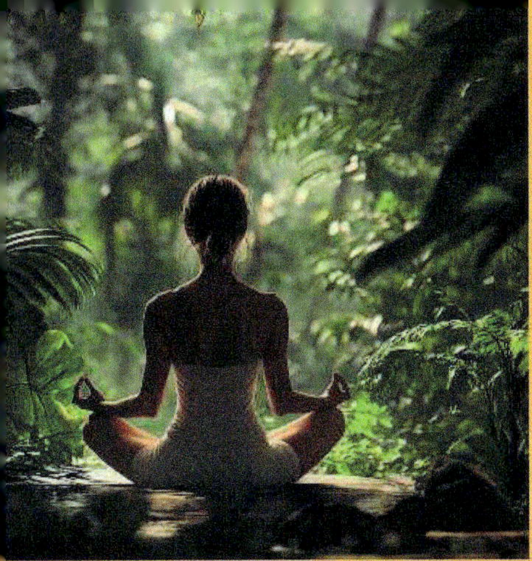
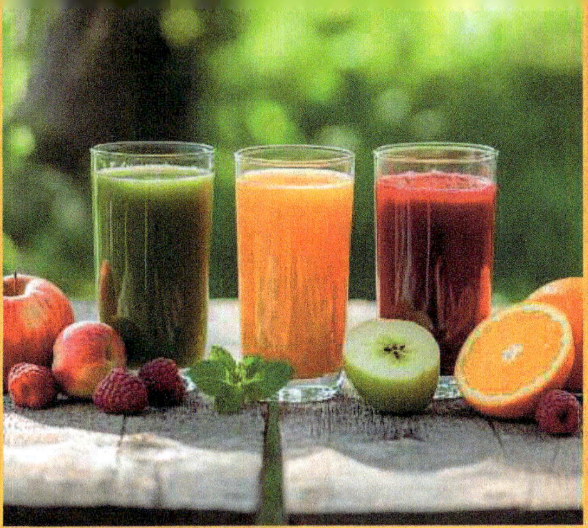
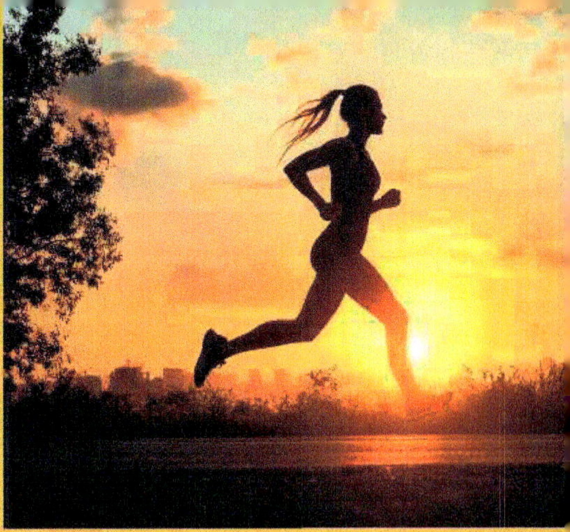
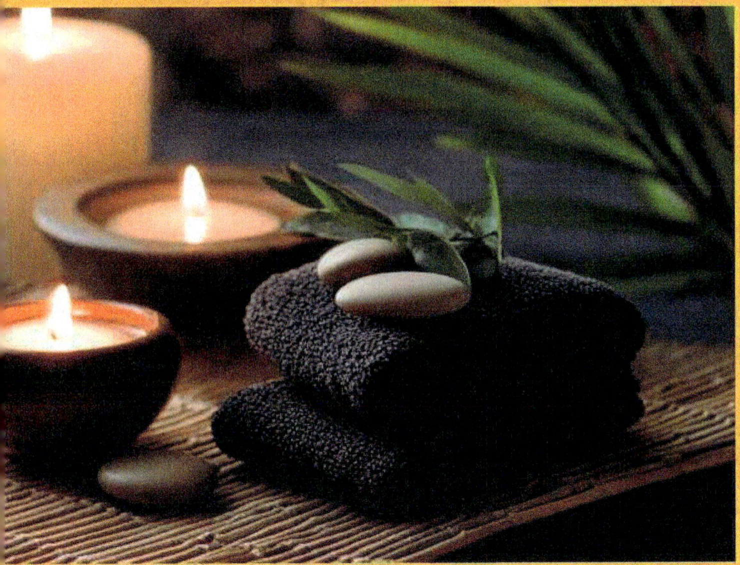
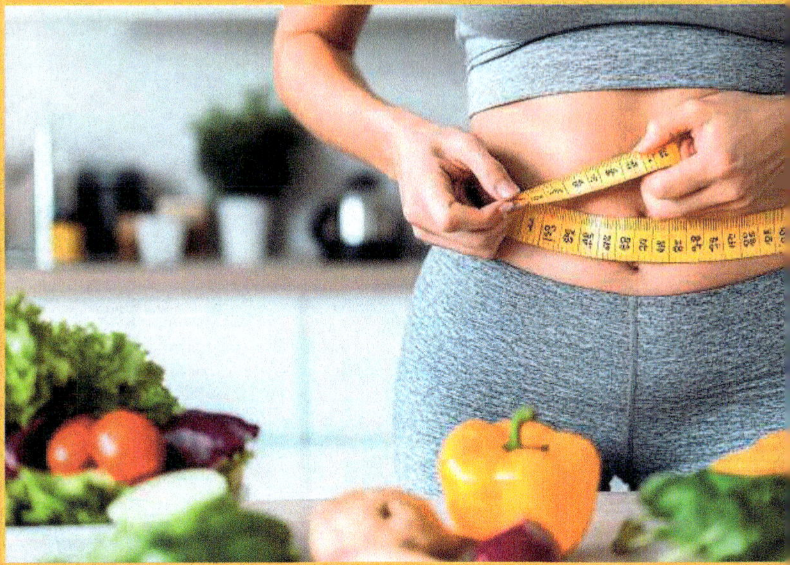
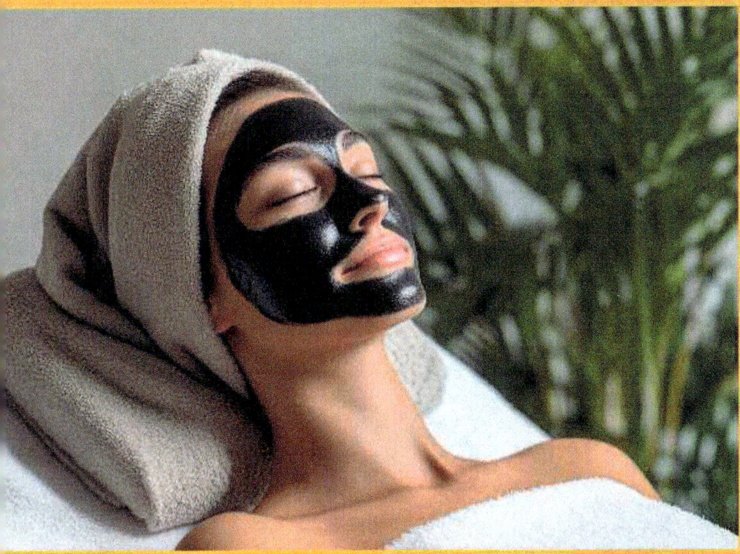
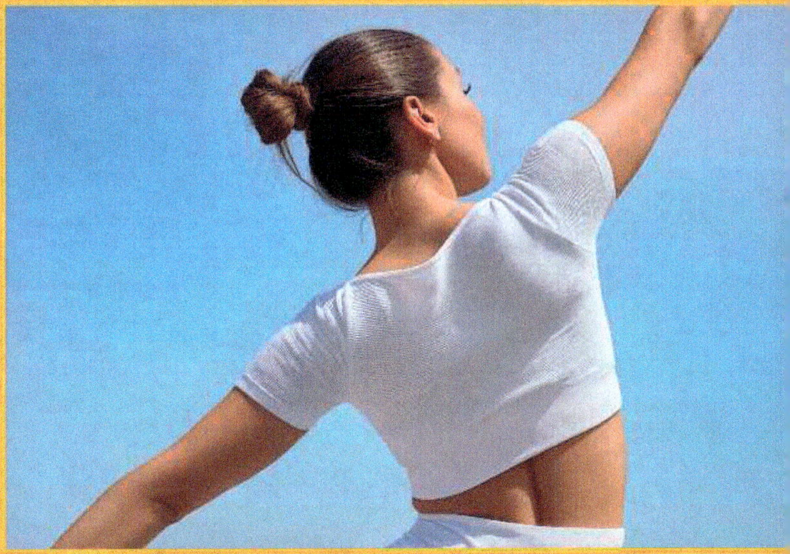
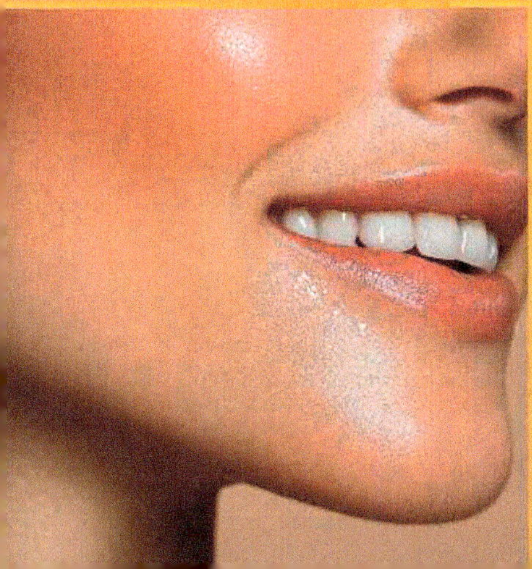
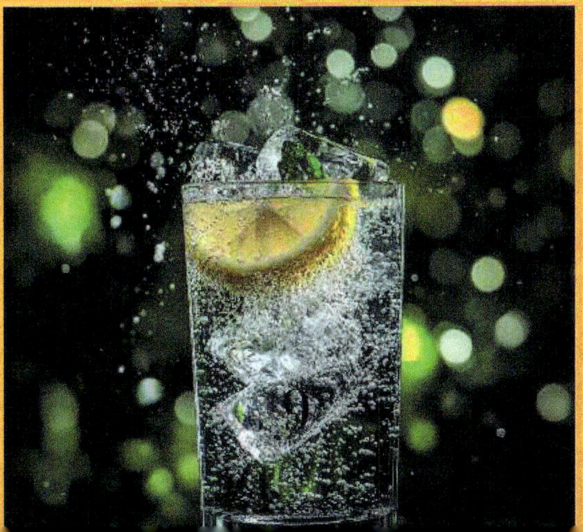
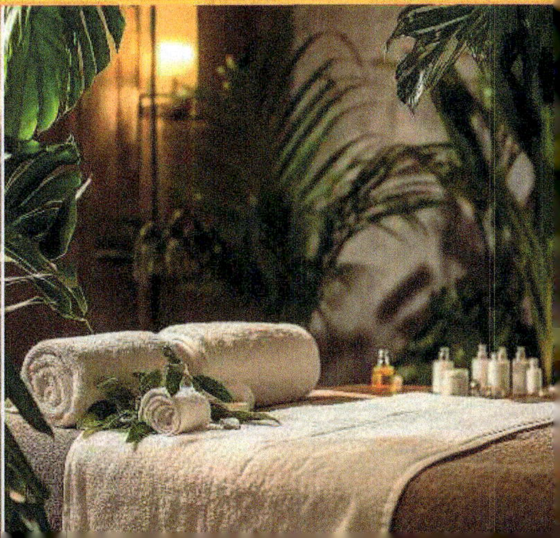

Health begins with harmony

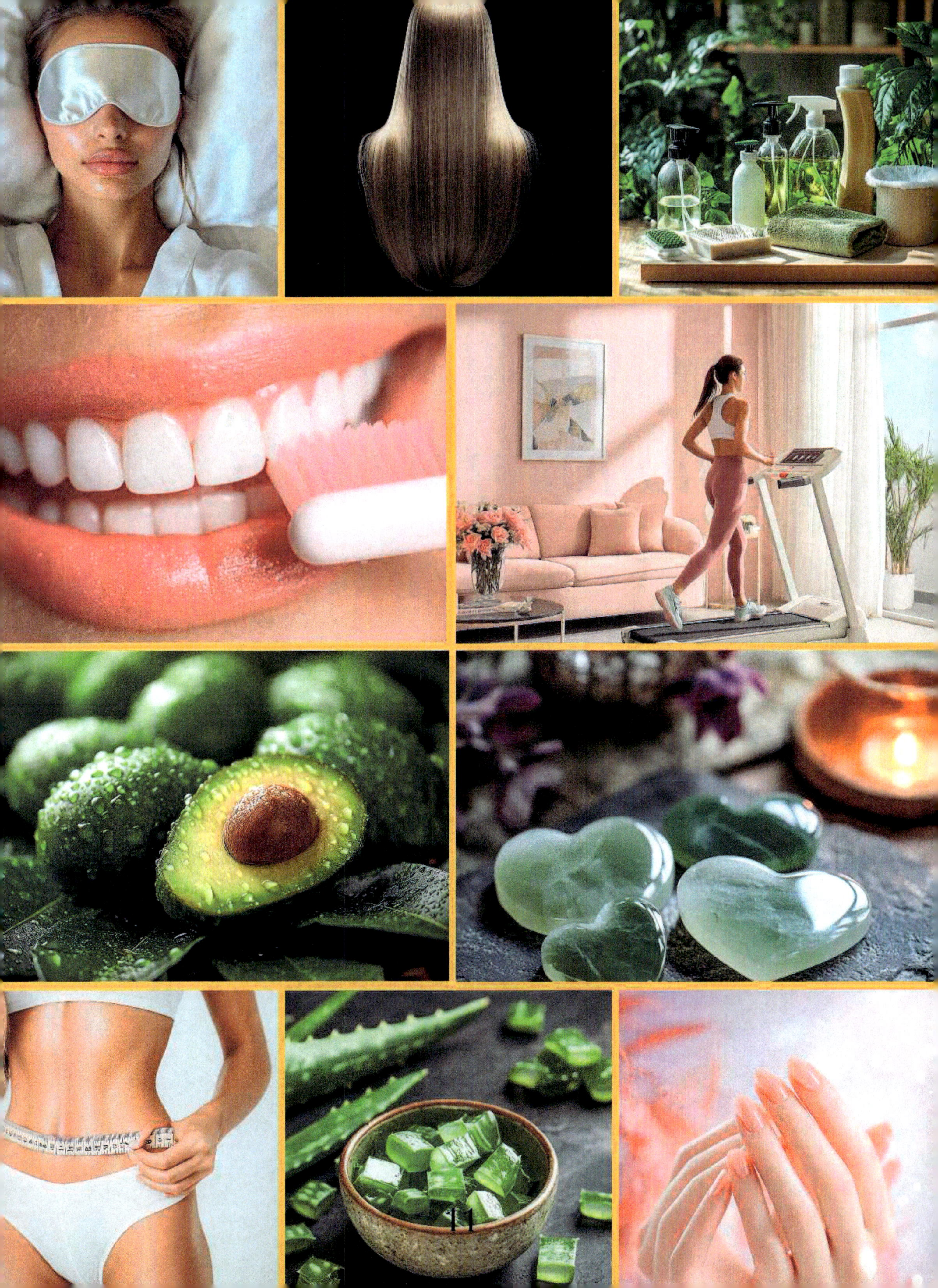

"This is not just a drink

-

It's a daily promise to honor my body."

Every choice I make a vote for the body, I love

Health
begins with harmony

My energy is sacred. I protect it, nourish it, and honor it

I fuel my body With purpose, not punishment

Movement is my celebration, not my obligation

I feel strong, vibrant, and fully alive

I listen to my body — It always knows

Rest is not a luxury — It's my power source

I am healing, glowing, becoming.	 My wellness is a priority, not a reward	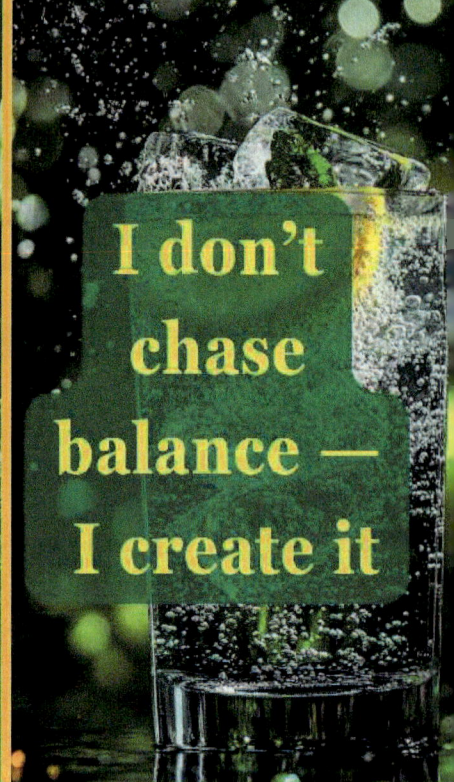 I don't chase balance — I create it
 Vitality is my natural state.	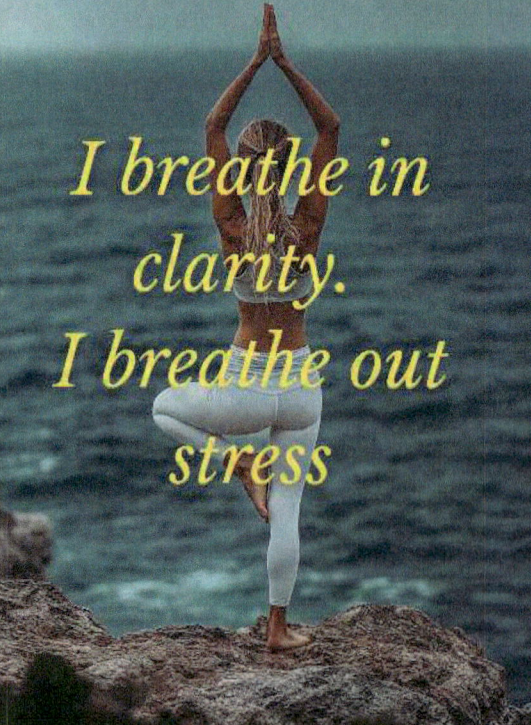 I breathe in clarity. I breathe out stress	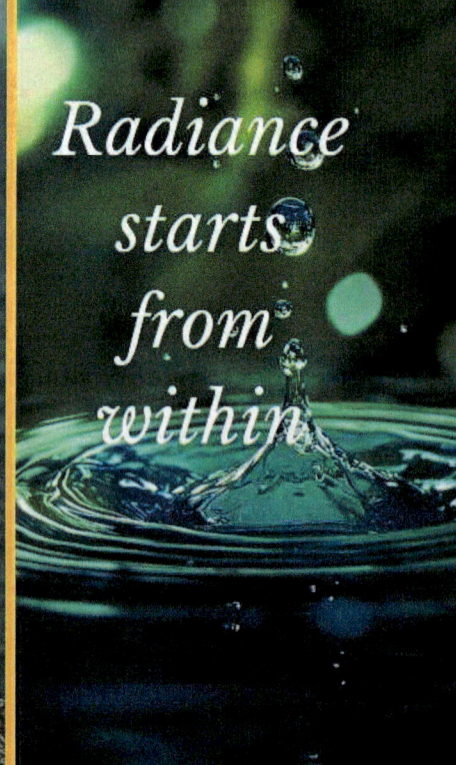 Radiance starts from within
 I honor my body. It carries me through my purpose		 I am the keeper of my energy

LOVE & ROMANCE

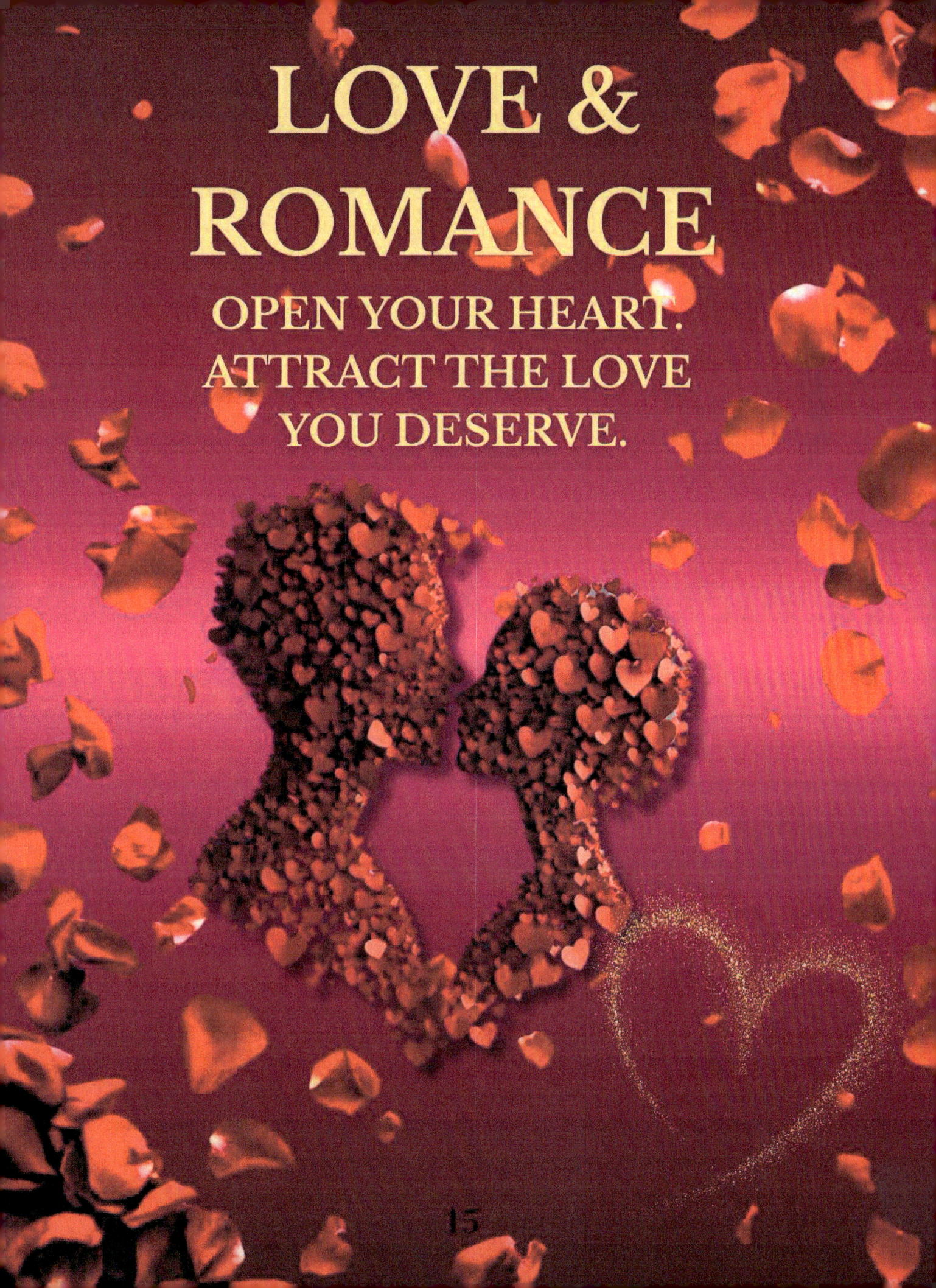

OPEN YOUR HEART. ATTRACT THE LOVE YOU DESERVE.

VISUALIZE THE LOVE YOU DESERVE

What does a fulfilling relationship look like to you? Is it a romantic partner, deep emotional connection, passion, or a life filled with mutual respect and joy? Visualizing love is about opening your heart and creating space for deep, genuine connection.

MOTIVATIONAL QUOTE:
"Love is not just something you feel — it's something you build."

HOW TO USE THIS SECTION
1. Picture Your Ideal Relationship
Choose images that reflect the type of love you want to attract:
Holding hands, candlelit dinners, traveling together, laughing in the kitchen.

2. Write Heartfelt Affirmations
Add phrases like:
– "I am worthy of love and affection."
– "I attract a relationship that uplifts and inspires me."
– "My heart is open to deep, soulful connection."

3. Set Romantic Intentions
Could you define your vision for love? Do you want to manifest a new relationship, deepen an existing one, or attract actual soulmate energy?

VISUALIZATION PRACTICE:
Take 5 quiet minutes each day:
– Close your eyes.
– Visualize the love you want to experience.
– Feel the joy, peace, and butterflies of being loved.
– Smile and feel your heart open to love.

LOVE ACTION TIPS
–Practice Self-Love: Treat yourself the way you want to be treated in a relationship.
– Make Space: Declutter your space and your mind to welcome love in.
– Be the Energy You Want to Attract: Radiate love, and love will find you.

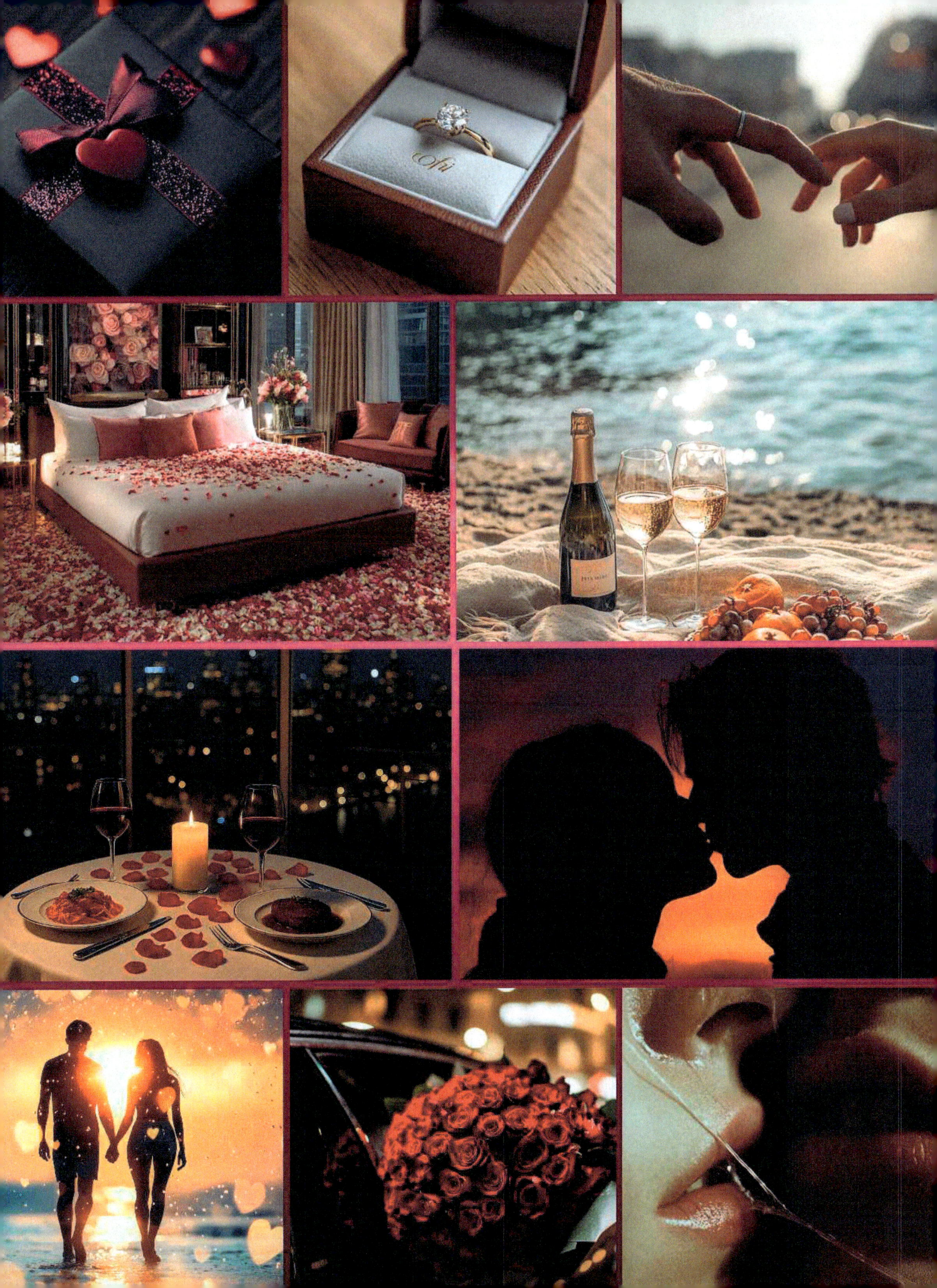

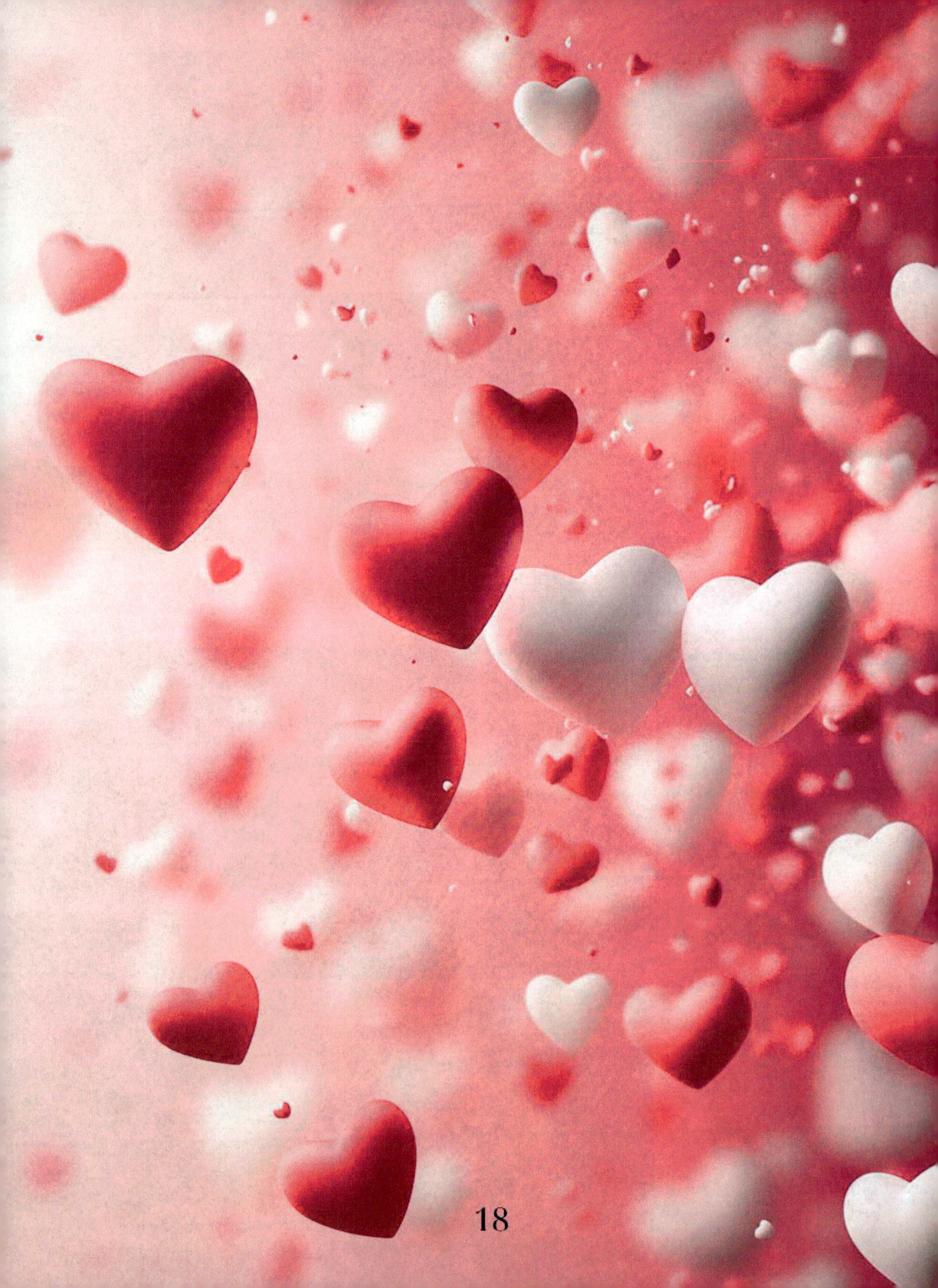

PS, love you.

I love love

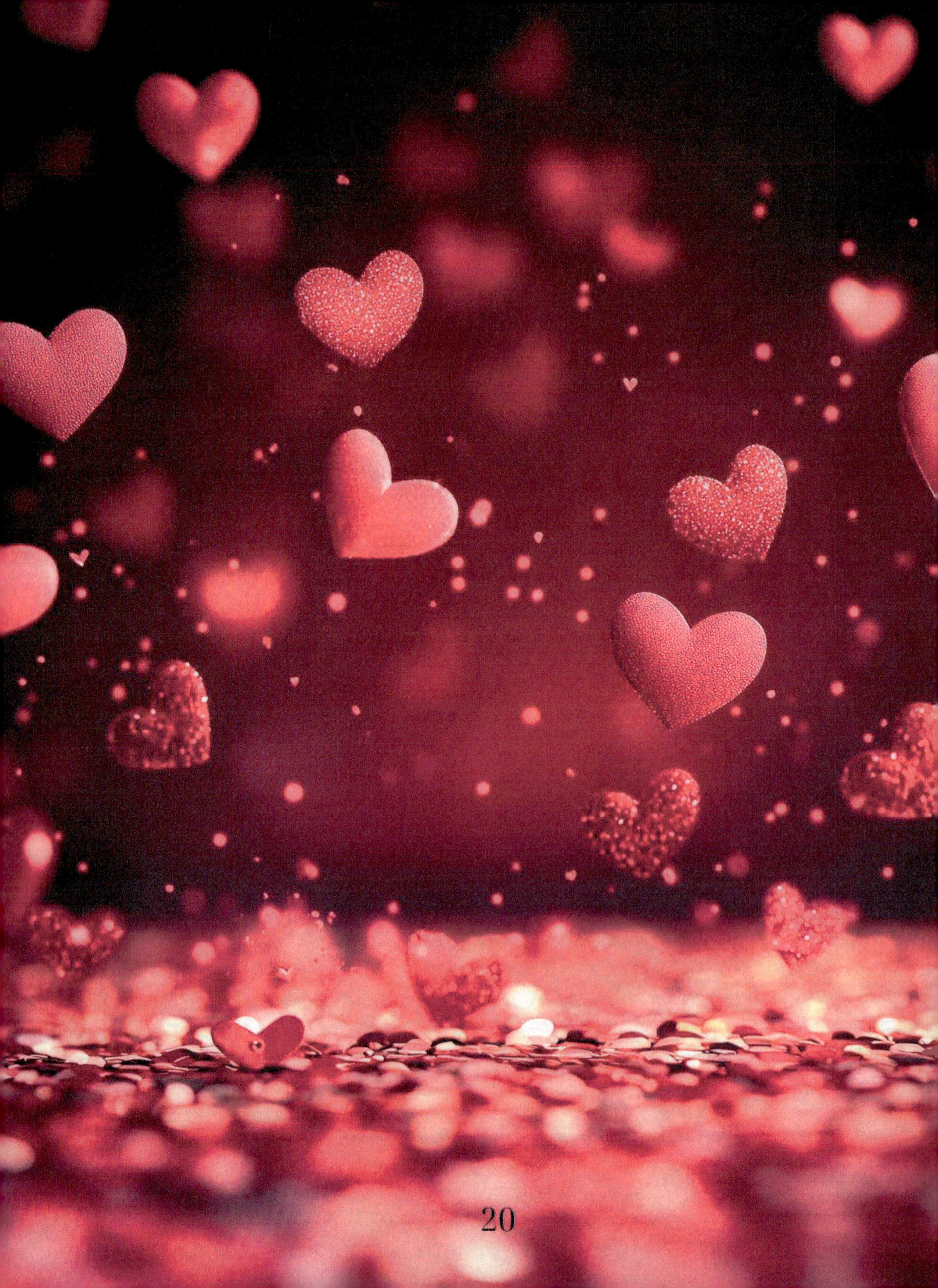

I attract a relationship built on truth, trust, and tenderness	REAL LOVE FEELS LIKE PEACE WRAPPED IN PASSION	I am open to love that nourishes my soul.
I deserve a love that feels like coming home	Our love is a sacred space — where we both grow and glow	The love I give is the love I receive — multiplied
Two hearts, one rhythm — That's us		I am worthy of extraordinary love

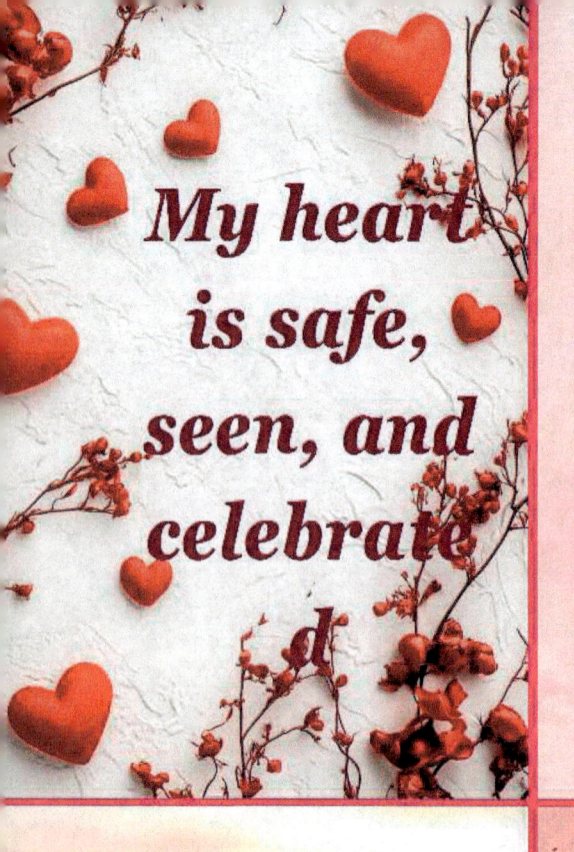

My heart is safe, seen, and celebrated	Love isn't about being perfect — it's about being real, together	We don't find love — we create it, every day
I radiate love — and it returns to me in divine timing	LOVE IS NOT A DESTINATION. IT'S HOW WE WALK TOGETHER	Romance lives in the little things
I don't chase love. I embody it		My relationship is filled with joy, laughter, and depth

FAMILY & ROOTS

WHERE LOVE BEGINS AND LEGACY LIVES ON

"Family is my foundation, my safe place, and my reason to rise."

VISUALIZE THE FAMILY LIFE YOU DESIRE

What does family mean to you? It might be the laughter around the dinner table, the strength of traditions, the comfort of being fully accepted, or the legacy you're building for generations to come. Visualizing family is about deep connection, belonging, and unconditional support.

MOTIVATIONAL QUOTE:
"Family is not just blood — it's the bond that shapes who we are."

HOW TO USE THIS SECTION

1. Honor Your Family Values
Choose images that represent love, support, shared traditions, and family gatherings. These visuals anchor your goals in emotional connection and belonging.

2. Create Affirmations for Connection
Say or write phrases like:
 – "My family is a source of strength and love."
 – "I honor my roots and cherish my loved ones."
 – "Together we grow stronger."

3. Visualize Your Family Dreams
What do you wish to manifest?
 – A loving partnership
 – Stronger bonds with parents, siblings, or children
 – Traditions that nurture generations
 – A home filled with joy

FAMILY REFLECTION PRACTICE:
Take a moment each evening to reflect on one meaningful family connection — past or present. Write a memory or gratitude thought in your journal. Let love for your family fuel your vision.

ACTIONABLE TIPS:
 – Reconnect: Call someone you miss.
 – Celebrate Traditions: Create a new one or revive an old one.
 – Pass it On: Share family stories with the next generation..

25

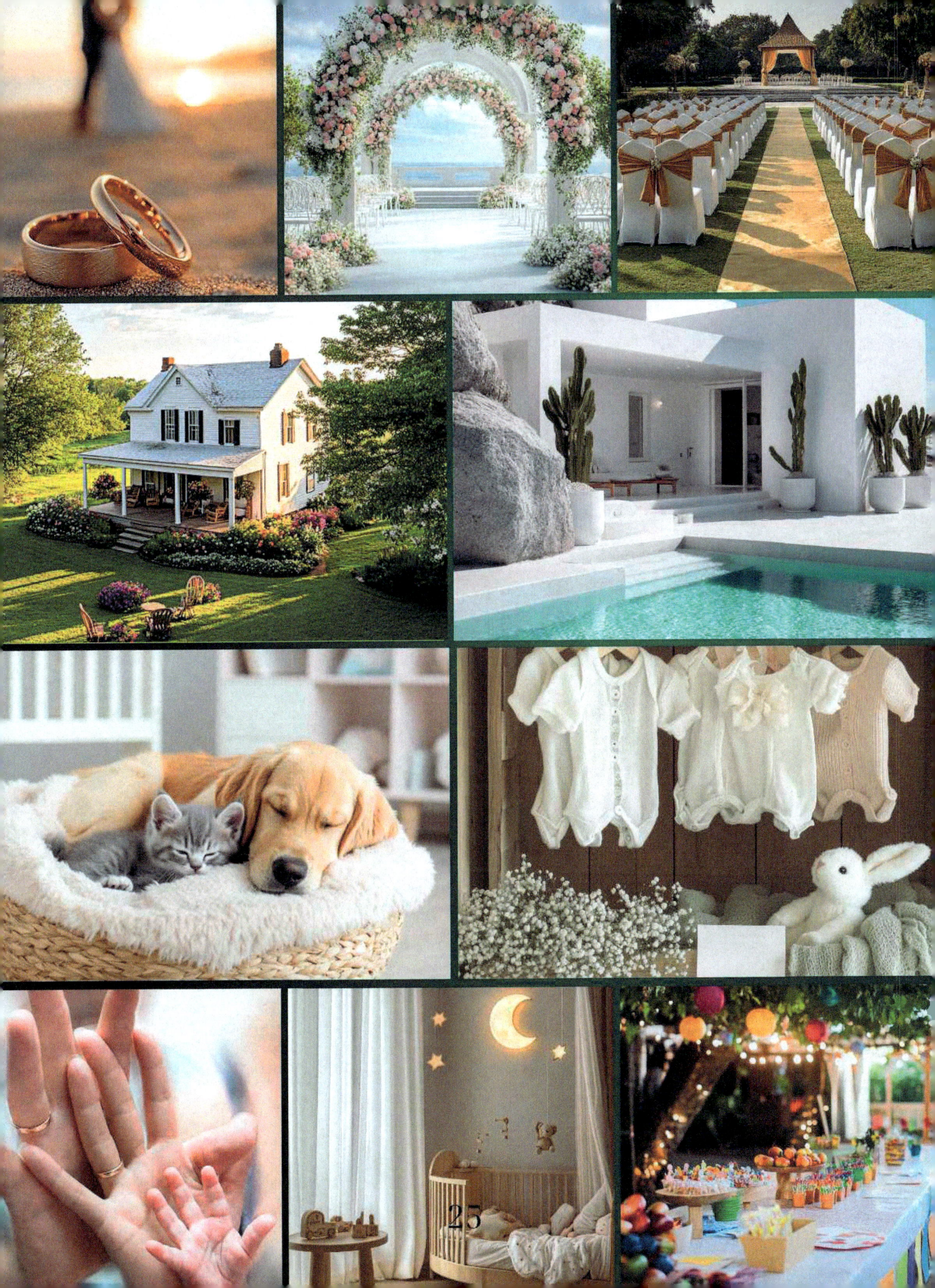

OUR FAMILY IS OUR STRENGTH

27

**THE FAMILY CREST
IS THE
SOULPRINT OF GENERATIONS.**

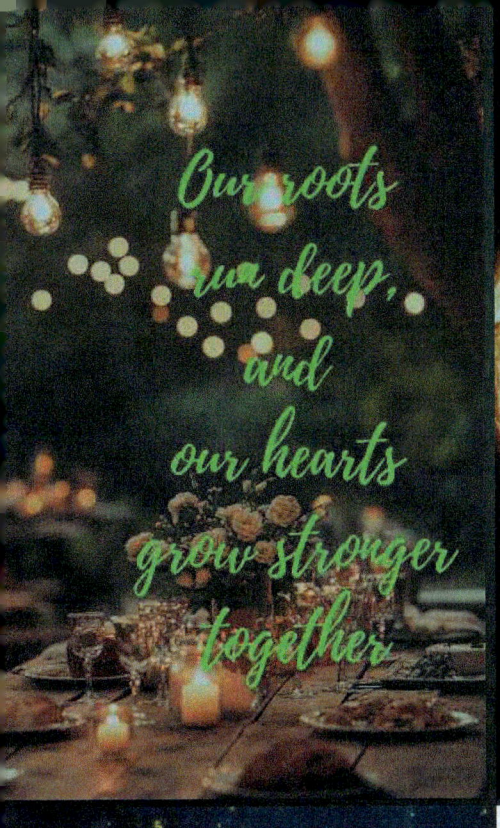

- Our roots run deep, and our hearts grow stronger together
- Roots that keep me grounded, love that lifts me higher 
- I nurture the future by honoring the past 
- I build a family where hearts are safe and dreams are shared 
- Family is where life begins, and love never ends 
- My family is my forever foundation 
- Together It's our favorite place to be 
- Family is my strength, my circle, my home

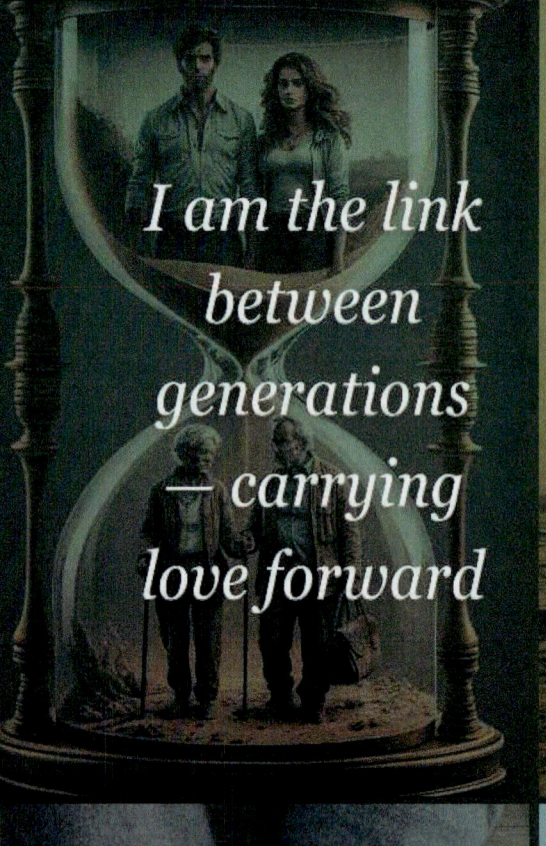

I am the link between generations — carrying love forward

Family isn't perfect, It's real — and that's where its power lives

The heart of my home beats with connection, laughter, and light.

Home
It is not a place. It's the feeling of being known and loved completely.

This love is generational and I am proud to carry it on

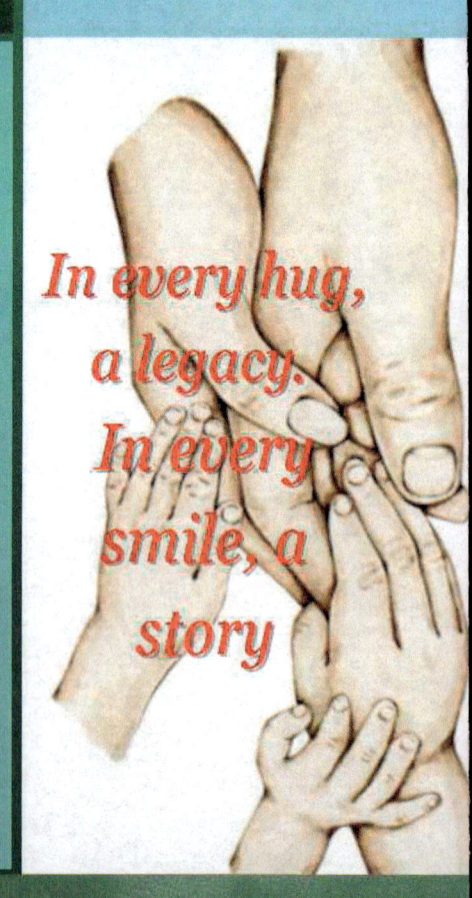

In every hug, a legacy. In every smile, a story

In this home, We grow with love, strength, and grace

Home is built with moments, not walls

FINANCES & WEALTH

BUILD YOUR WEALTH

Financial GOALS

Abundance ZONE

Debt-Free LIFE

VISUALIZE YOUR FINANCIAL FREEDOM

MOTIVATIONAL QUOTE:
"Your wealth can be an instrument for freedom, fulfillment, and success."

HOW TO USE THIS SECTION
Choose images that symbolize success:
- Debt-free statements
- Thriving businesses
- Passive income
- Your dream home

CREATE ABUNDANCE AFFIRMATIONS
Add phrases like:
- I am financially free.
- Money flows easily and joyfully into my life.
- I am open to limitless wealth.

SET FINANCIAL MILESTONES
WRITE YOUR 1-YEAR GOALS:
- Savings target
- Income boost
- Debt reduction
- Investment plans

VISUALIZATION PRACTICE
Manifesting Abundance
Take 5 quiet minutes each morning:
- Close your eyes.
- Visualize yourself receiving payments, watching your account grow, or celebrating a financial win.
- Engage your senses: hear the "payment received" sound, feel the excitement, see the number in your bank account.
- Smile. You are already attracting abundance.

ACTIONABLE WEALTH TIPS
Master Your Money
Track your daily spending to uncover hidden patterns and unlock smarter choices.
Invest in Growth
Choose books, courses, and mentorships that elevate your mindset and multiply your value.
Embrace Your Abundance
Repeat daily: "I am worthy of unlimited wealth, success, and joy."

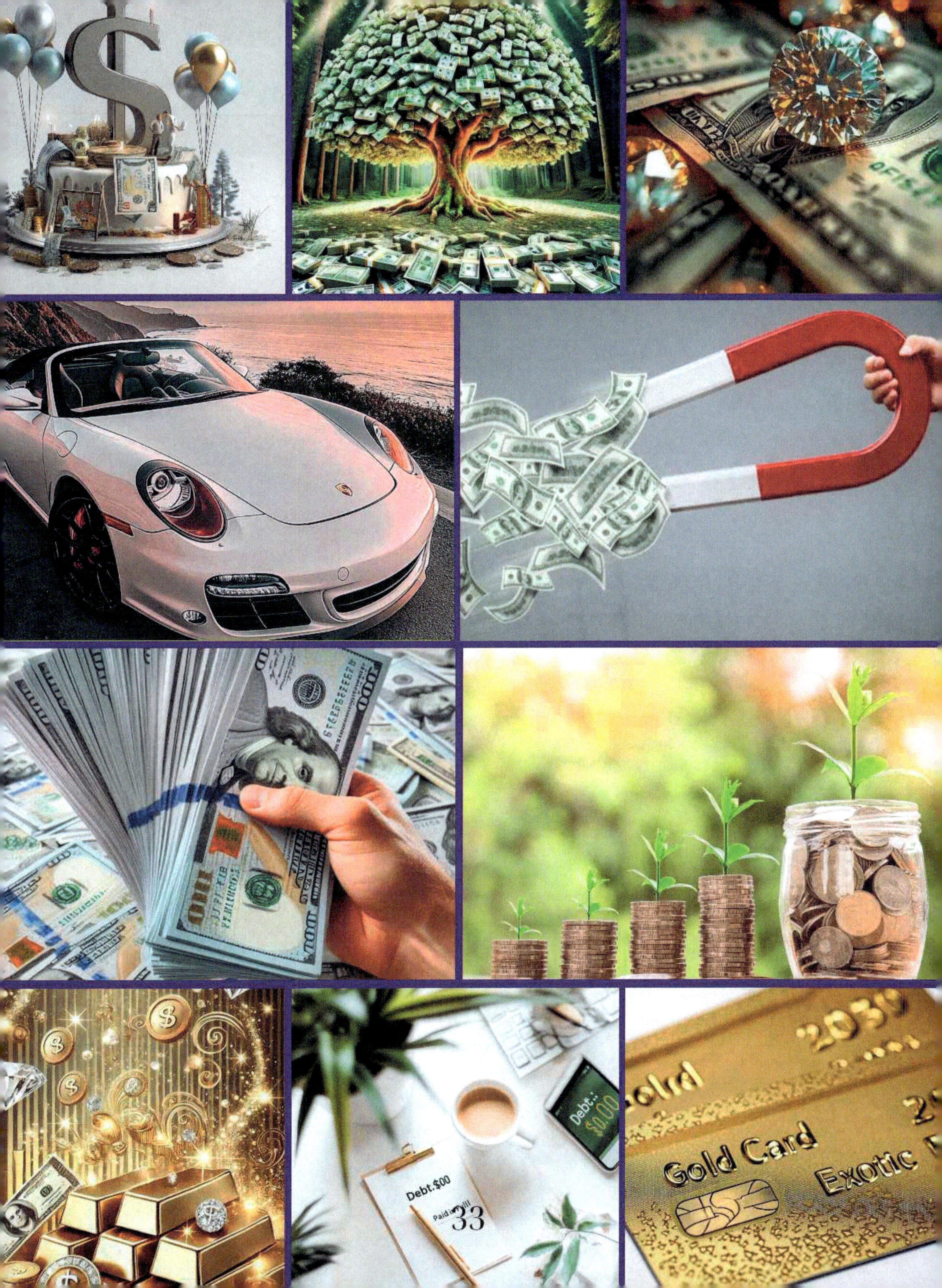
Debt.$00
33
Gold Card

MONEY
LOVES ME,
And I love it.

MY INCOME GROWS CONSISTENTLY.

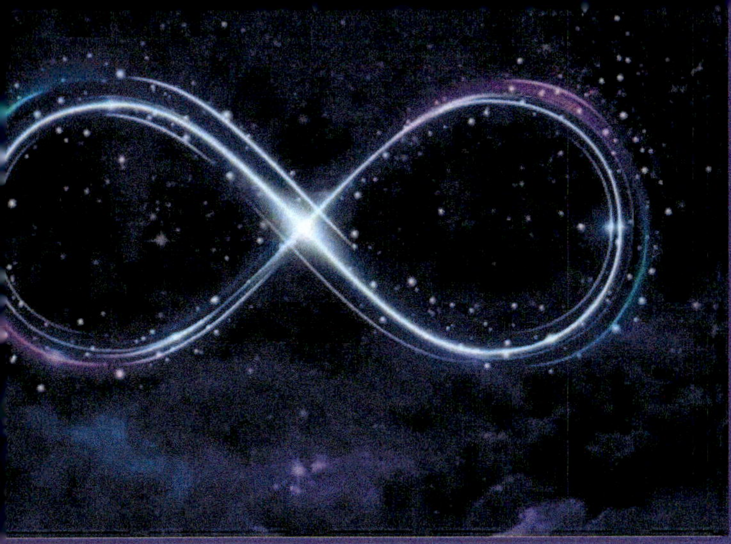

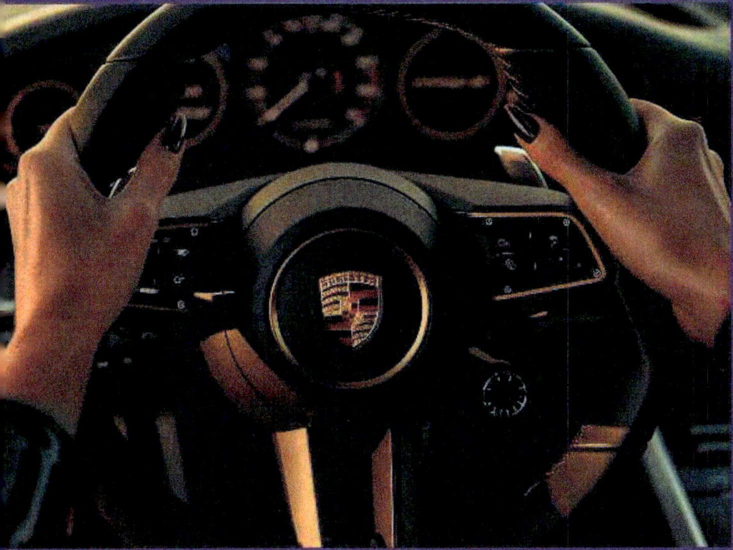

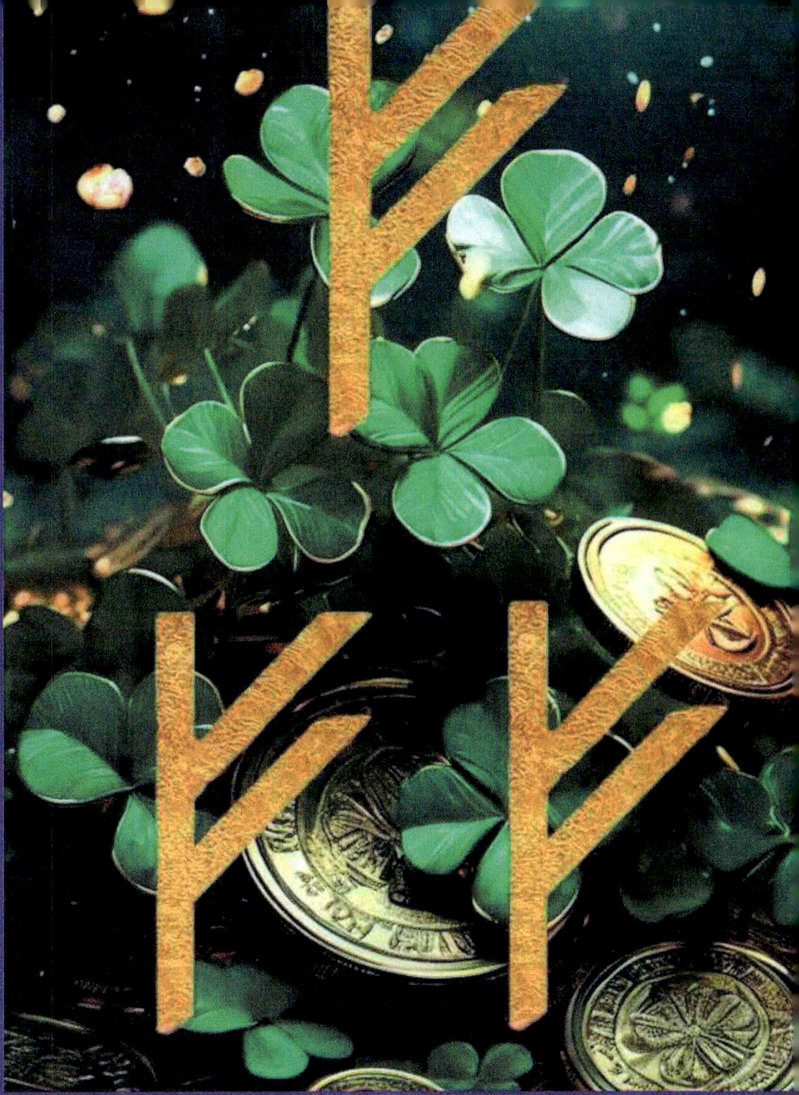

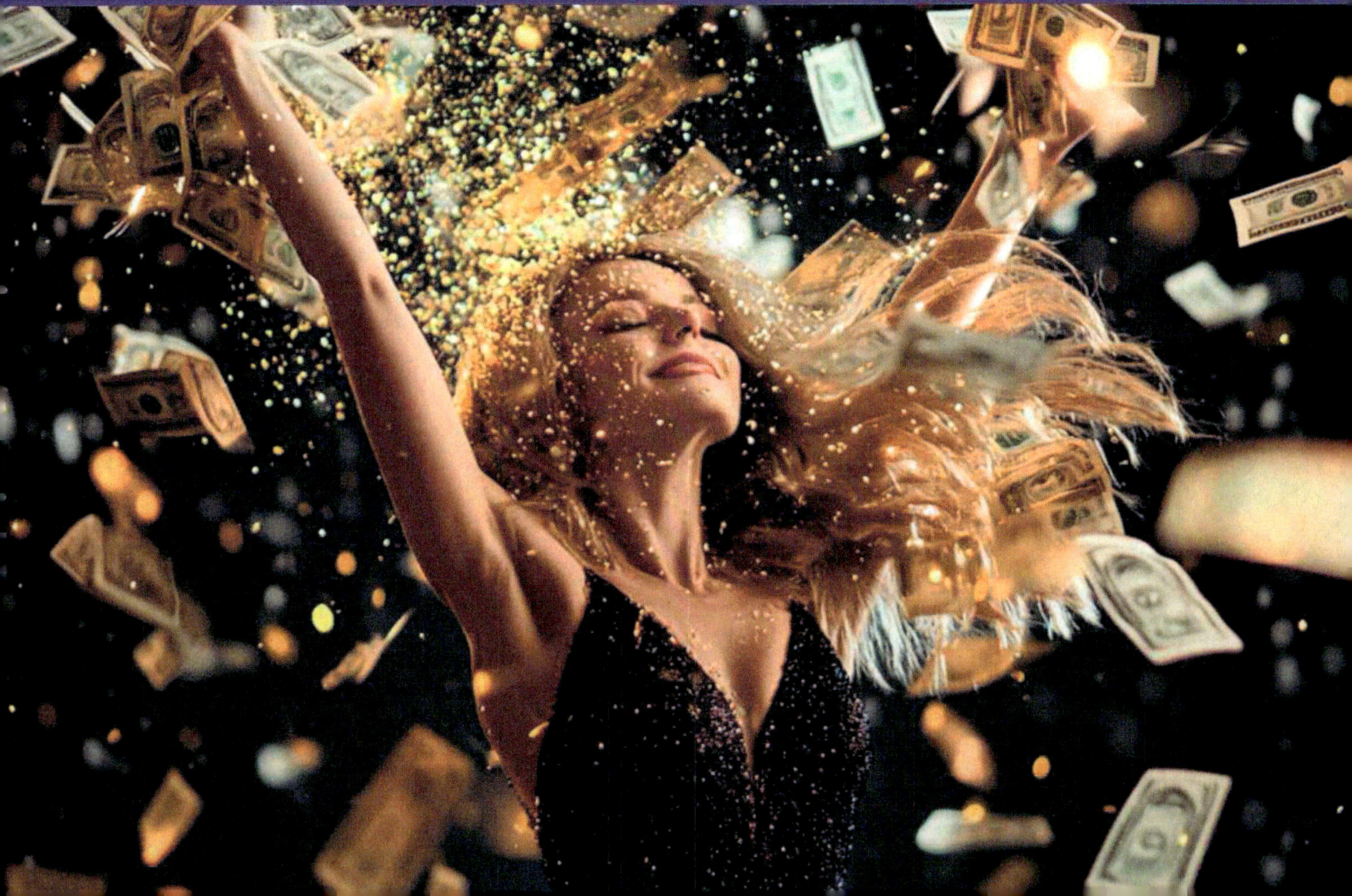

DATE _____

PAY TO THE
ORDER OF _____ $ _____

DOLLARS _____

MEMO _____   _____

Your name _____   0123

Date _____ 20 ___

Pay to the order of _____ $ _____
_____ dollars

Memo _____   _____

:012345678 :0123 :01234

36

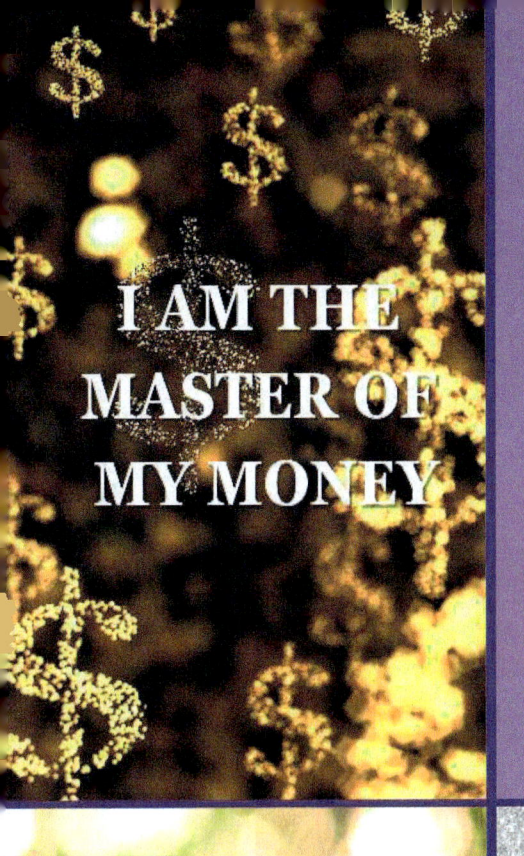

I AM THE MASTER OF MY MONEY	**I CREATE INCOME DOING WHAT I LOVE**	*Wealth flows to me from multiple sources*
I am financially empowered and focused	**I am open to receiving limitless abundance**	**MONEY IS A TOOL, AND I USE IT WISELY**
I INVEST IN MY FUTURE EVERY SINGLE DAY	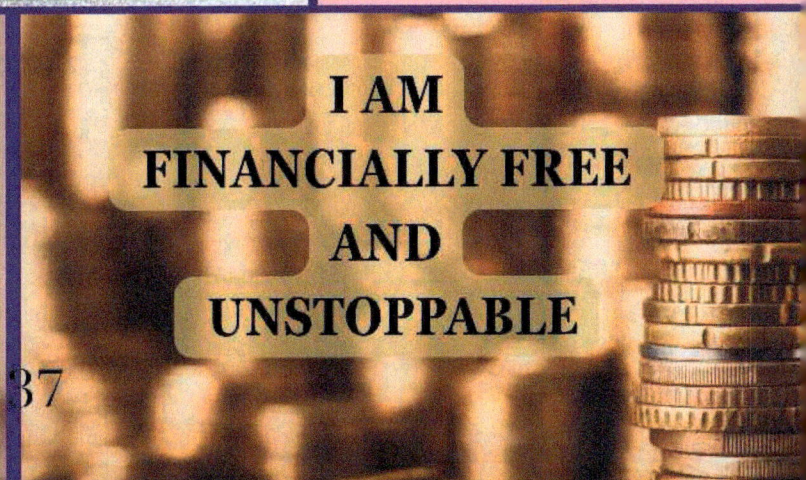	**I AM FINANCIALLY FREE AND UNSTOPPABLE**

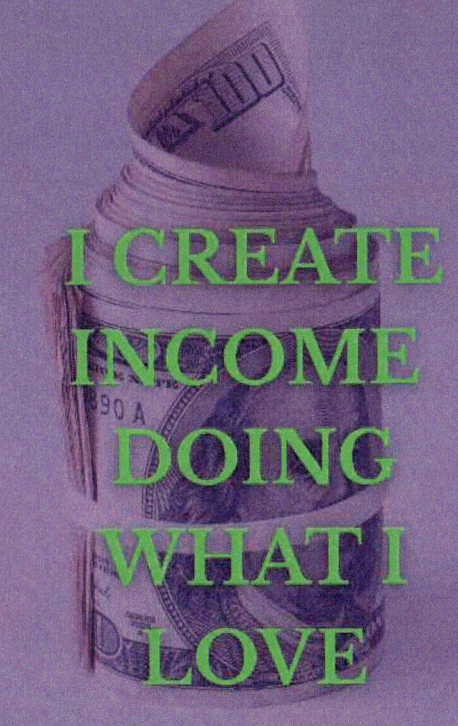

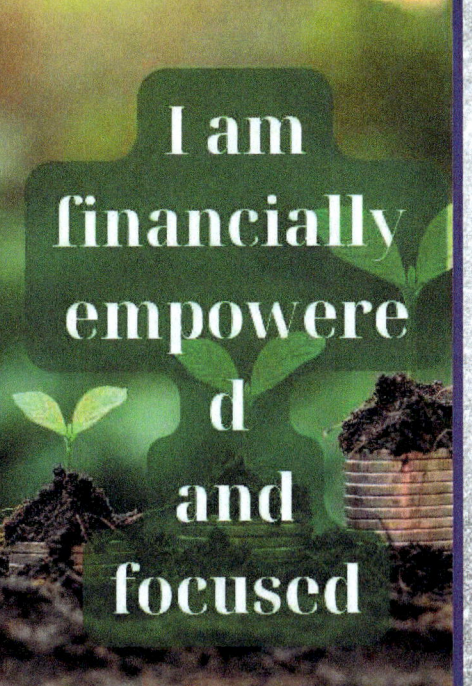

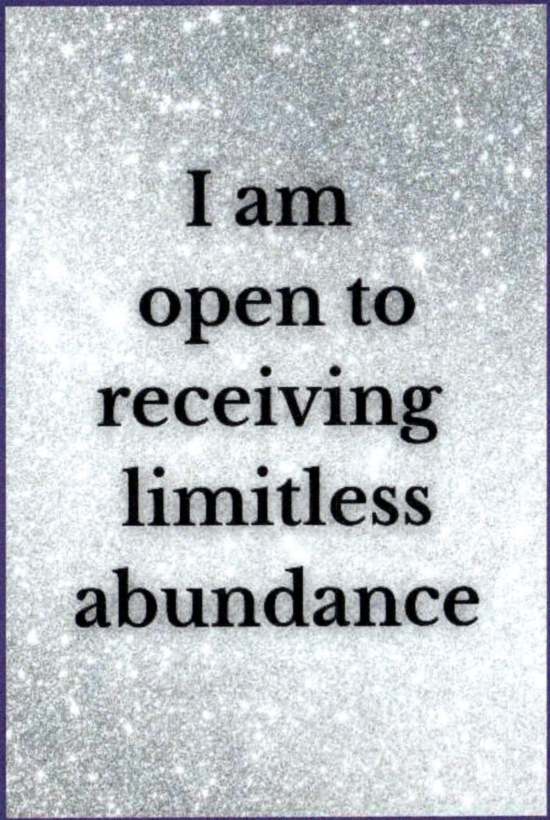

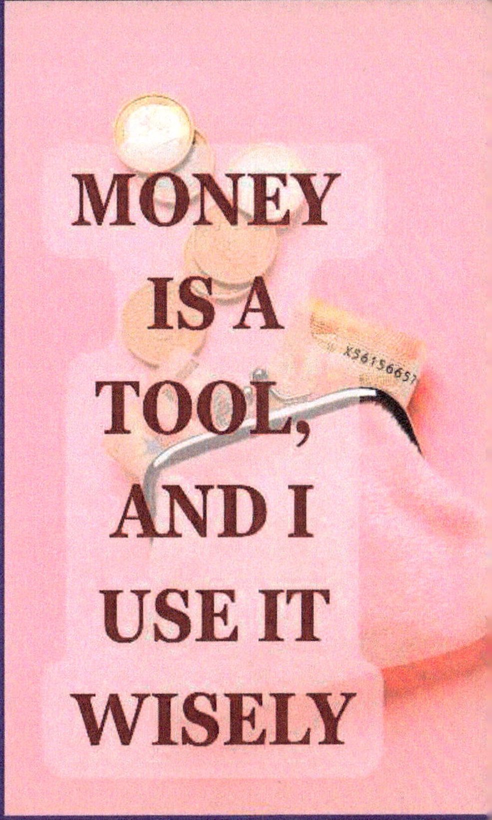

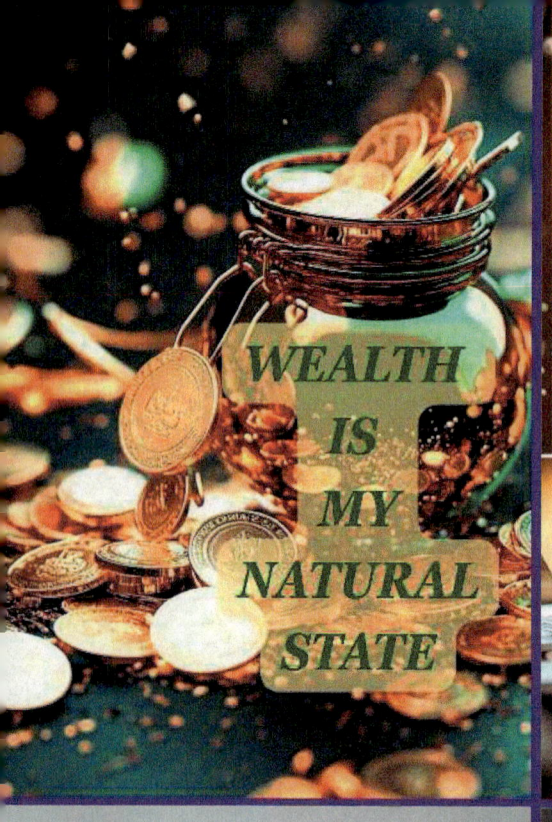

WEALTH IS MY NATURAL STATE	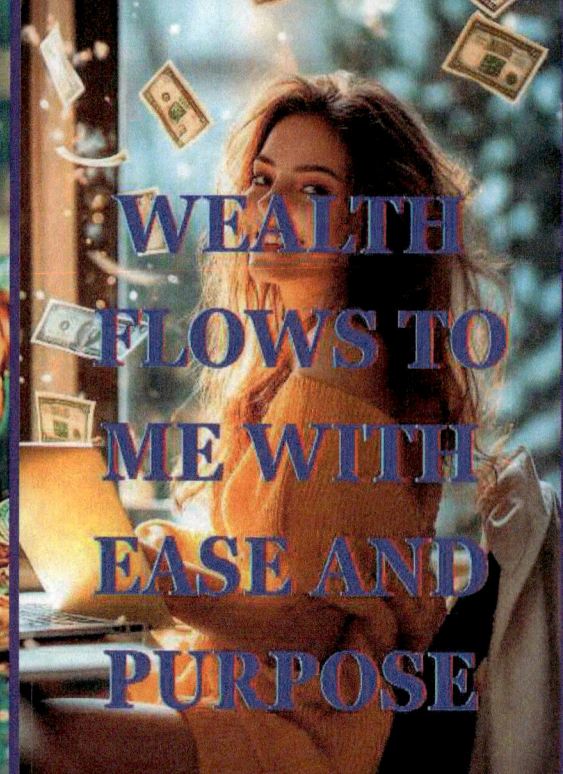 WEALTH FLOWS TO ME WITH EASE AND PURPOSE	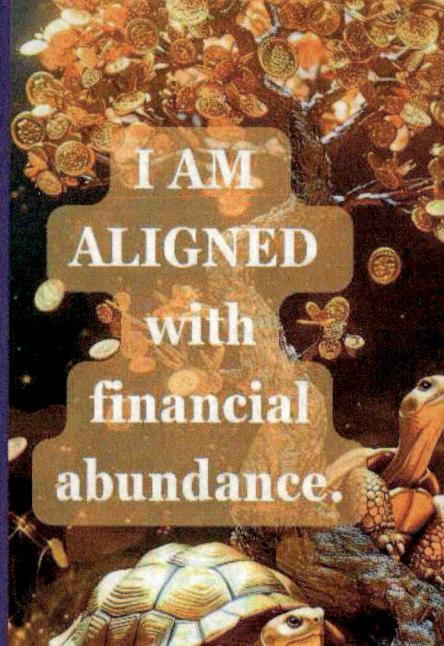 I AM ALIGNED with financial abundance.
 Abundance isn't luck — it's my mindset	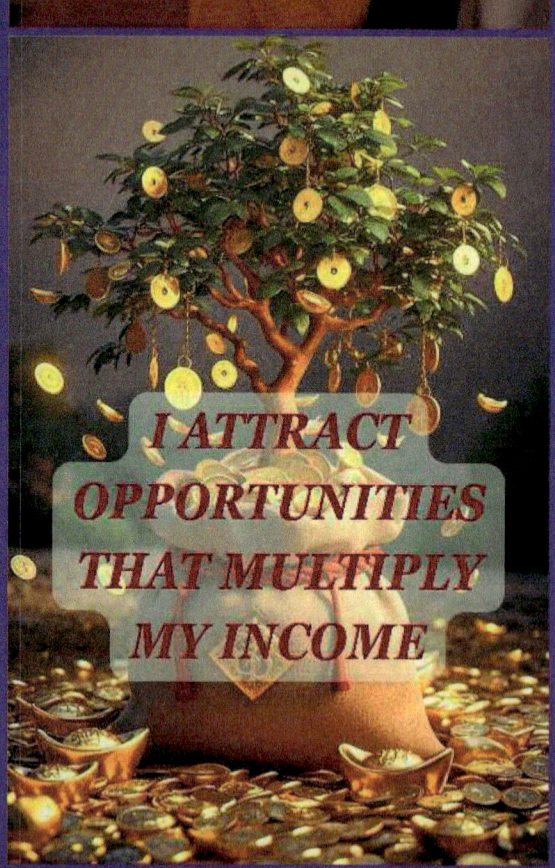 I ATTRACT OPPORTUNITIES THAT MULTIPLY MY INCOME	 MONEY IS A TOOL I USE TO CREATE FREEDOM, IMPACT, AND JOY
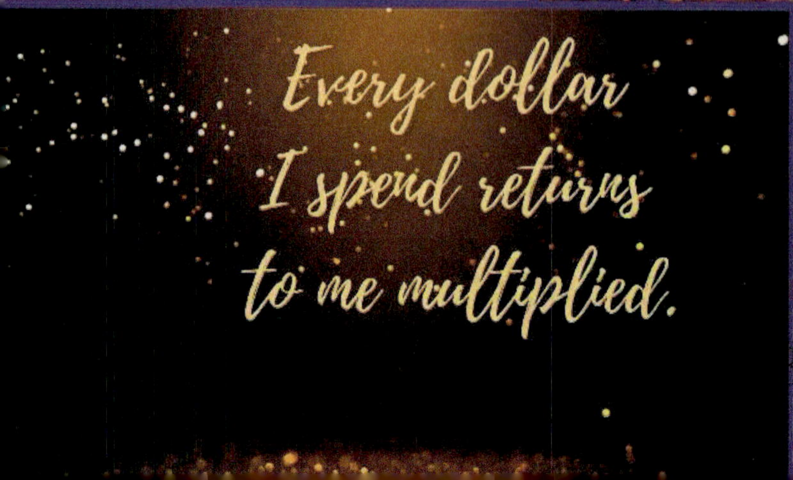 Every dollar I spend returns to me multiplied.		 I AM THE CREATOR OF MY FINANCIAL REALITY

FAME & RECOGNITION

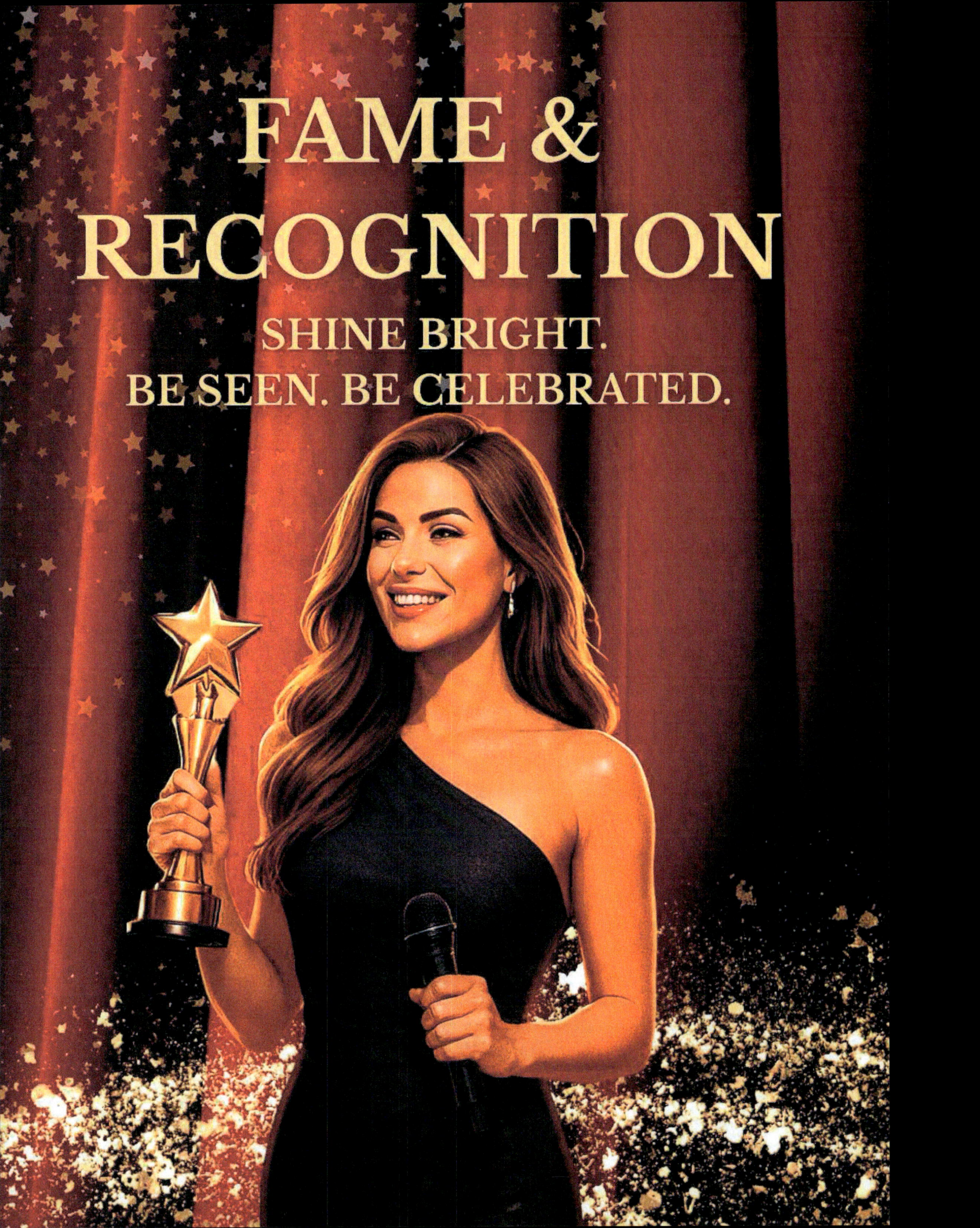

SHINE BRIGHT.
BE SEEN. BE CELEBRATED.

VISUALIZE YOUR MOMENT IN THE SPOTLIGHT

What does recognition mean to you? Is it a standing ovation, your name on a door, a bestselling book, or the confidence to speak up and be heard? Recognition is about impact. It's the moment your work, voice, or presence is celebrated by others — and by yourself.

MOTIVATIONAL QUOTE:
"I was born to shine. And the world is ready for my light."

HOW TO USE THIS SECTION
Visualize Your Rise to Recognition
Choose images that represent success:
Spotlight moments, public speaking, published work, awards, or features.

CREATE EMPOWERING AFFIRMATIONS
Use phrases like:
– "I am recognized and respected."
– "My voice is powerful and inspiring."
– "I am seen, valued, and celebrated."

SET VISIBILITY GOALS
Write down your 1-year milestones:
– Launch my personal brand
– Speak at an event
– Be featured in media or a podcast
– Get acknowledged or rewarded for my wor

VISUALIZATION PRACTICE:
Take 5 minutes to see yourself in the spotlight:
– Imagine the applause, the lights, the energy.
– Feel the pride in being seen and heard.
– Let your body remember the sensation of standing tall.
– Smile. You're already magnetic.

ACTIONABLE VISIBILITY TIPS:
– Build your personal brand: authenticity = influence.
– Say yes to opportunities that scare and excite you.
– Share your story. People are waiting to hear it.
– Celebrate yourself now — not just later.

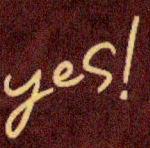

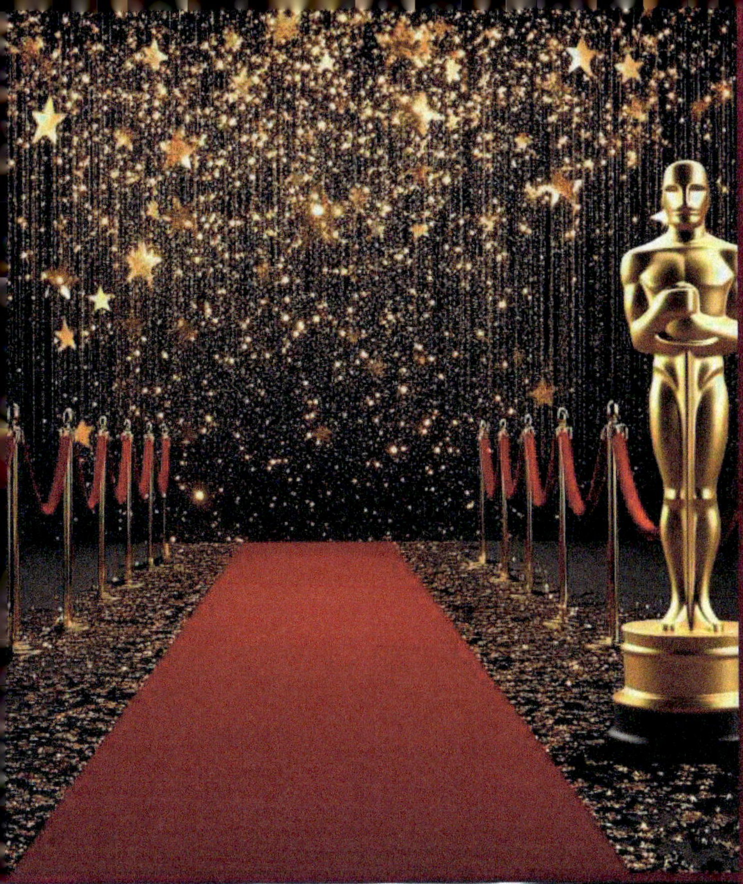

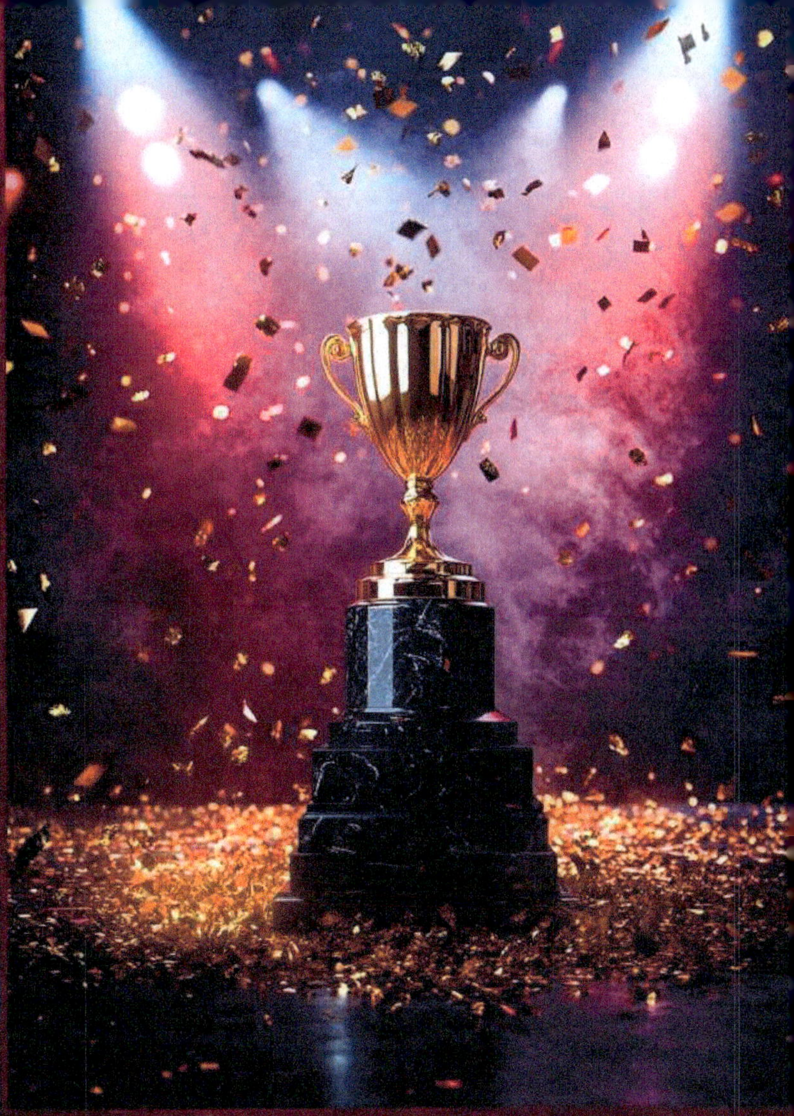

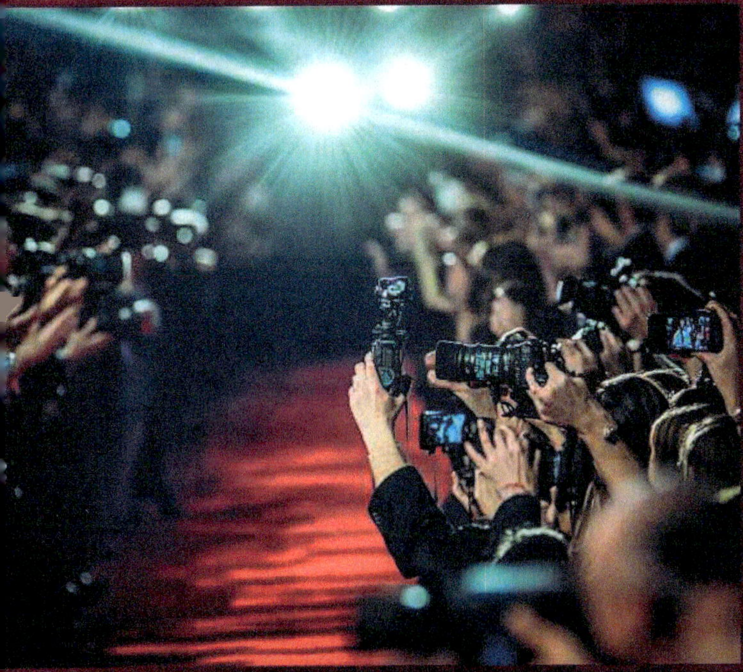

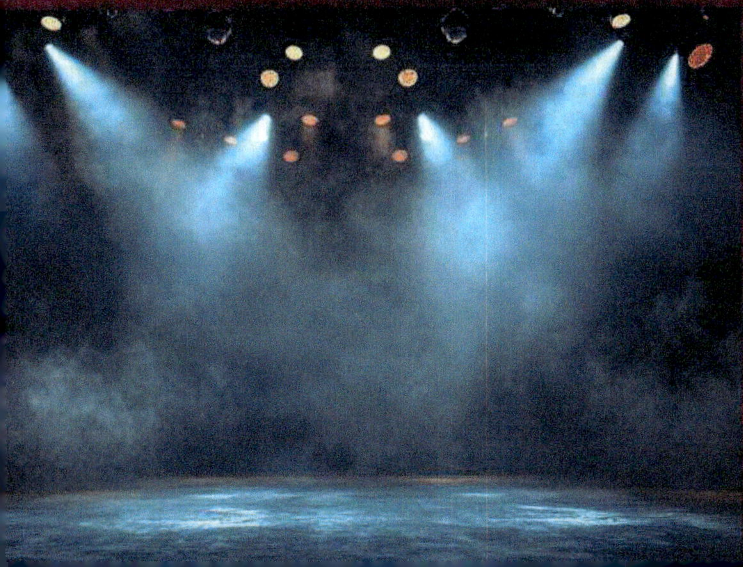

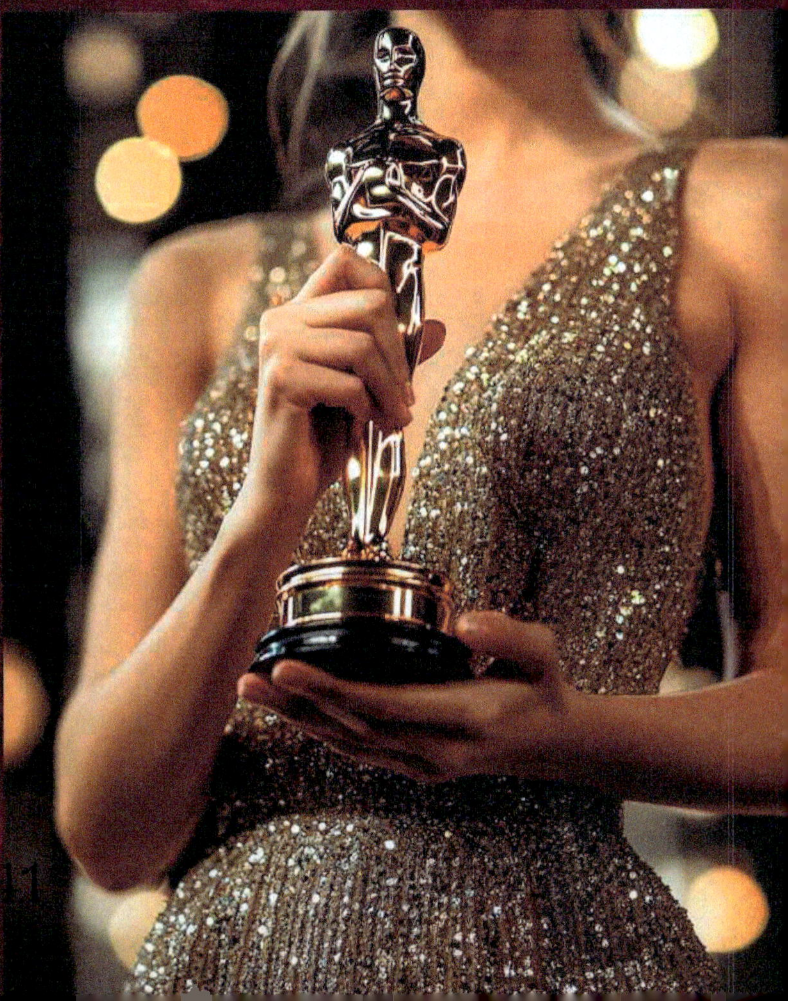

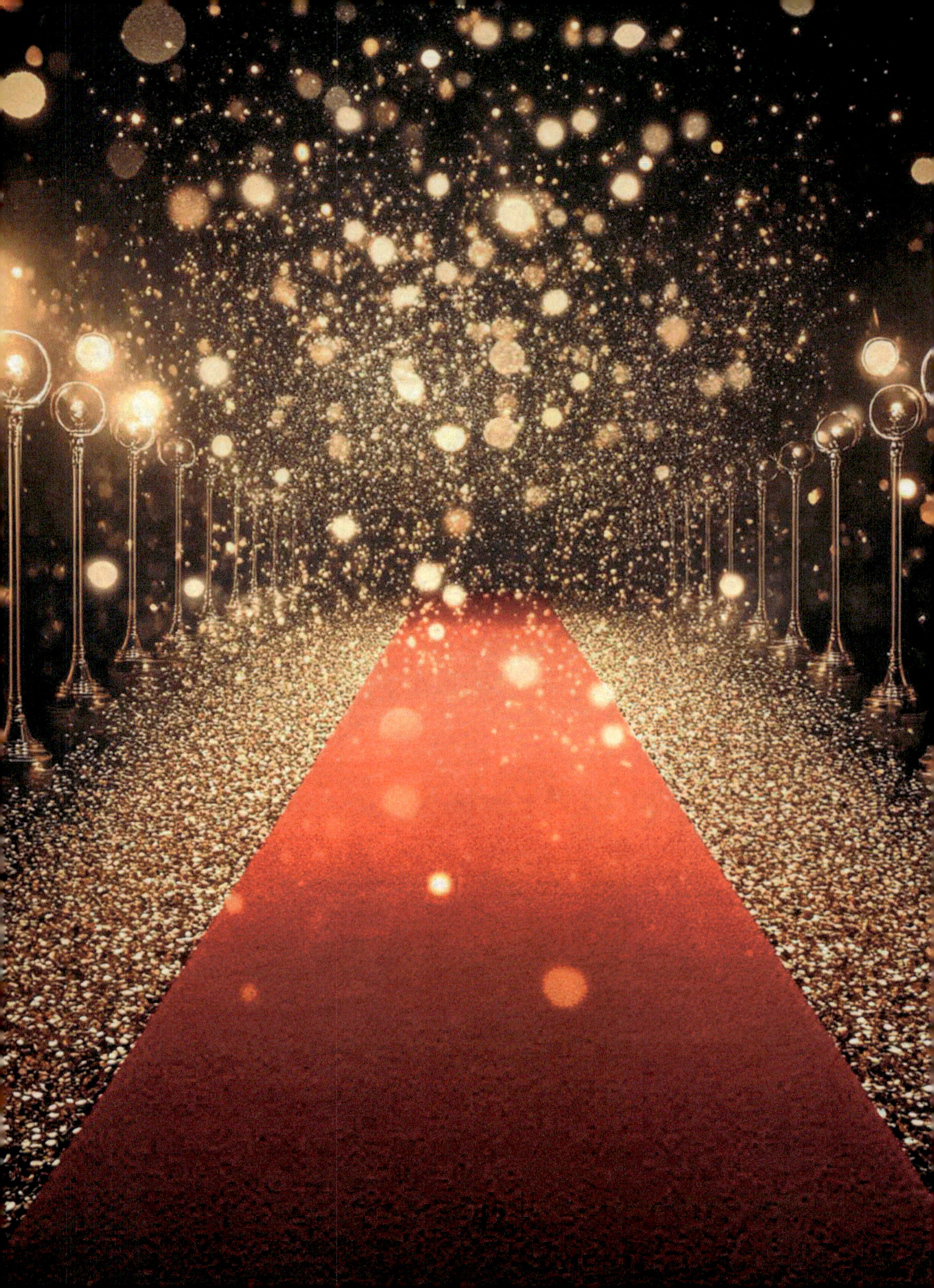

My Spotlight Moment

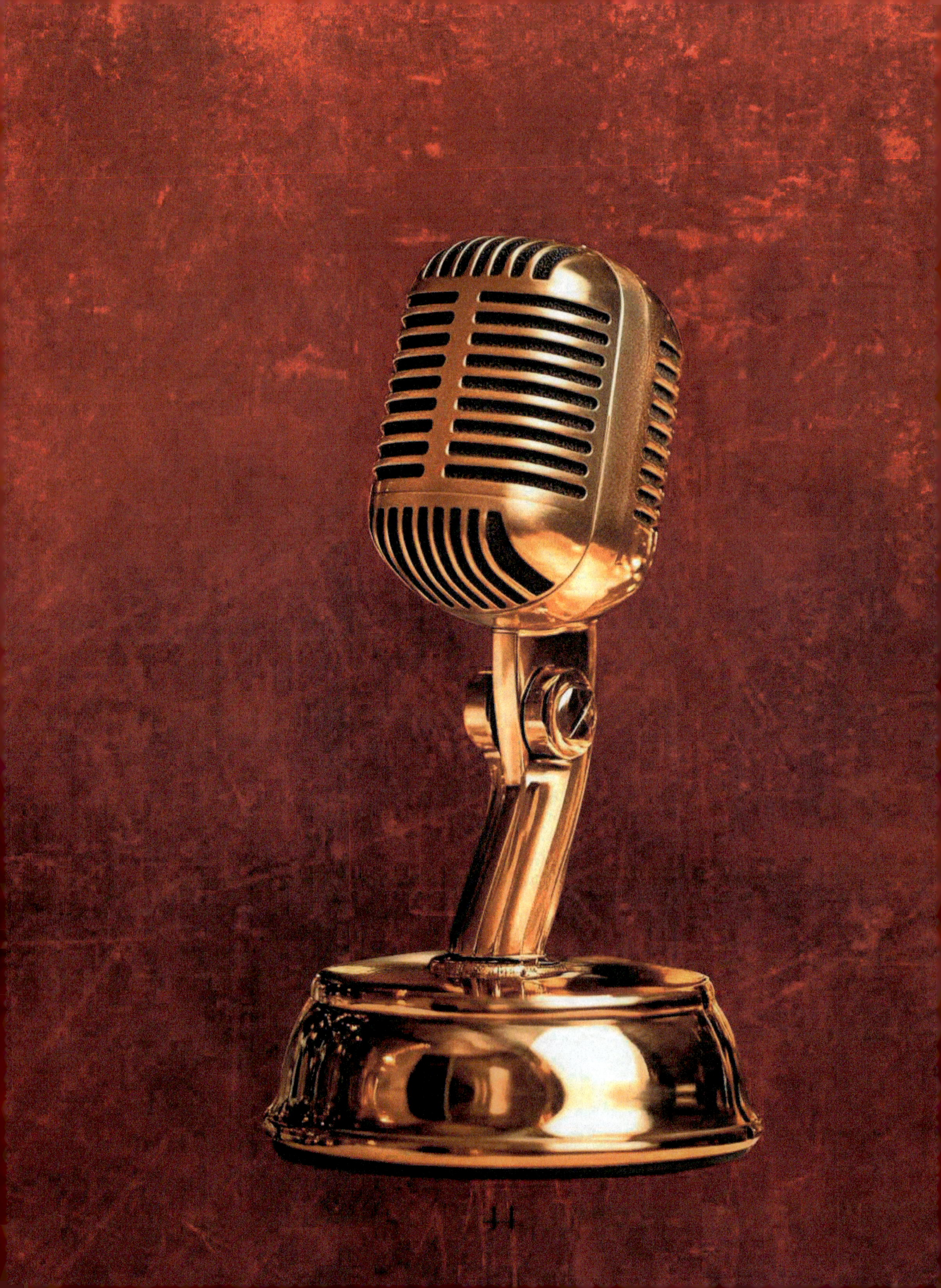

I wasn't made to dim. I was born to blaze	MY LIGHT ISN'T FOR DECORATION - IT'S FOR DIRECTION
I'M NOT WAITING TO BE DISCOVERED — I'M HERE TO BE REMEMBERED	LIGHTS. VISION. LEGACY
	MY LIGHT DOESN'T DIM — IT INSPIRES OTHERS.
I'M NOT JUST SEEN — I'M FELT	MY MOMENT TO SHINE
I don't just take the stage — I own the moment.	

- VISIBILITY IS NOT VANITY. IT'S PURPOSE WITH PRESENCE
- I DON'T SEEK APPLAUSE. I CREATE ECHOES
- I'M NOT PERFORMING — I'M BECOMING
- MY NAME IS SPOKEN IN ROOMS I HAVEN'T EVEN ENTERED YET
- I AM FEARLESS — THAT'S WHY FAME FOLLOWS ME
- I AM THE BRAND. I AM THE MOMENT. I AM THE LEGACY
- BUILT FOR THE SPOTLIGHT
- I DON'T CHASE FAME — IT NATURALLY FINDS ME.

CREATIVITY & CHILDREN

WHERE IMAGINATION BEGINS, AND WONDER NEVER ENDS

VISUALIZE THEIR
BRIGHTEST FUTURE

Motivational Quote
"Through creativity, children speak the language of their soul."

How to Use This Section
Visualize a World of Creative Growth:
What does creativity mean to you and your child? Is it messy finger painting on a sunny afternoon, bedtime stories filled with dragons and fairies, or building castles out of cardboard and dreams?

Use this section to explore the magic of creativity — and the joy of nurturing it, both in yourself and your little ones.

Affirmations to Inspire:
- "I create space for creativity to grow."
- "Together, we turn ideas into magic."
- "My child is an artist of imagination."
- "Play is sacred. Joy is learning. Mess is welcome."
- "Creativity connects our hearts."

Inspiring Images to Include
- *Crayons, paints, scissors, colorful paper*
- *Little hands painting or building something*
- *A cozy, magical reading nook*
- *A messy table full of creativity*
- *A child dancing, playing dress-up, or inventing a game*
- *Soft toys, musical instruments, illustrated books*
- *Parent & child creating side by side*

Visualization Practice: Spark Their Imagination
Take a deep breath.
Picture a warm space where joy lives — a table filled with color, your child's laughter echoing through the room, tiny hands discovering the world through color, shape, and sound.
You're not just raising a child — you're raising a thinker, a feeler, a creator.
See their eyes light up with pride as they show you what they made.
And remember: in every moment of play, a dream is forming.

Creative Habits to Manifest
- Create together — often and playfully
- Celebrate messy, magical moments
- Say yes to imagination
- Make space for daily self-expression
- Encourage curiosity and wonder
- Let their ideas lead the way

49

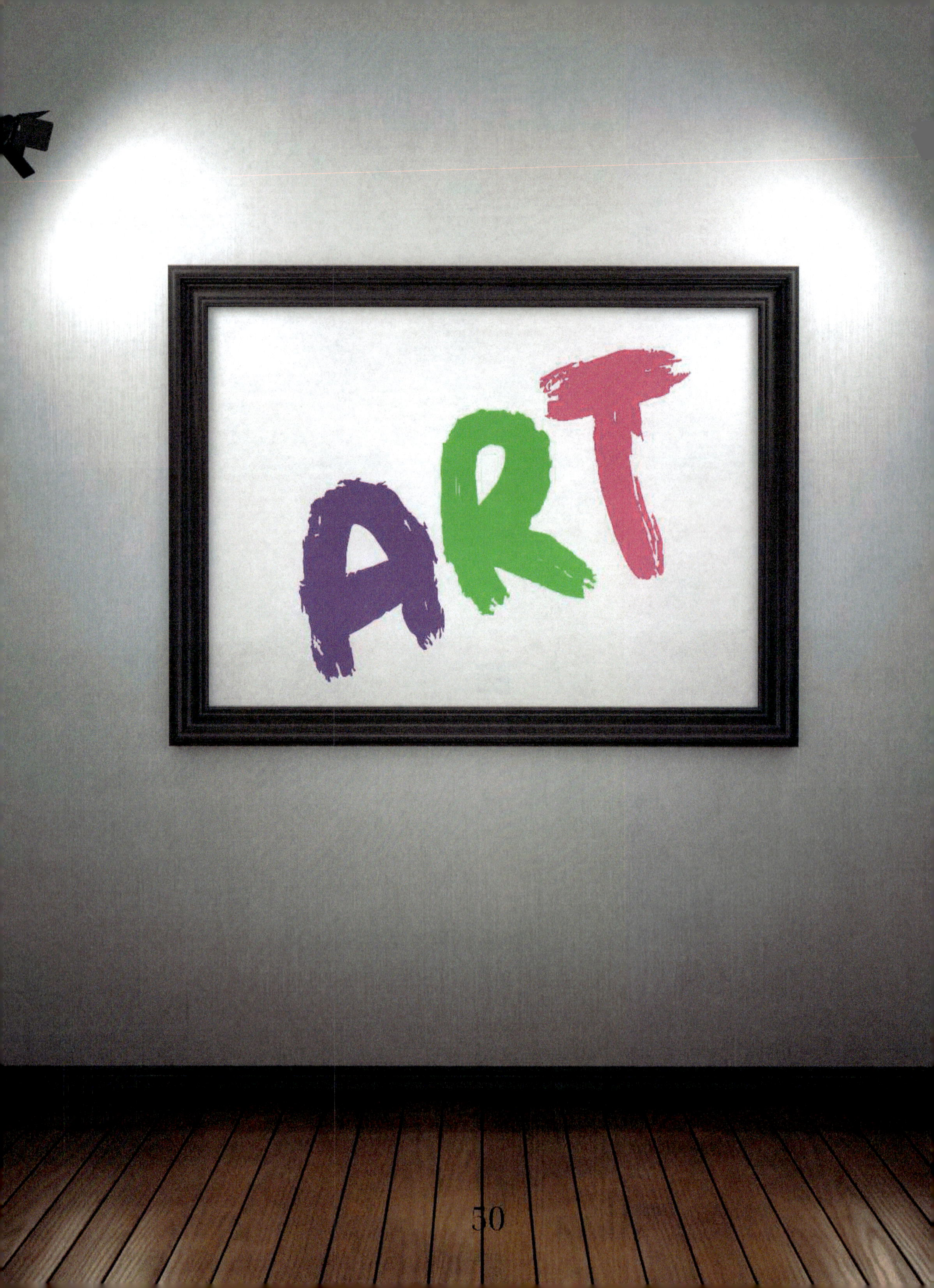
ART

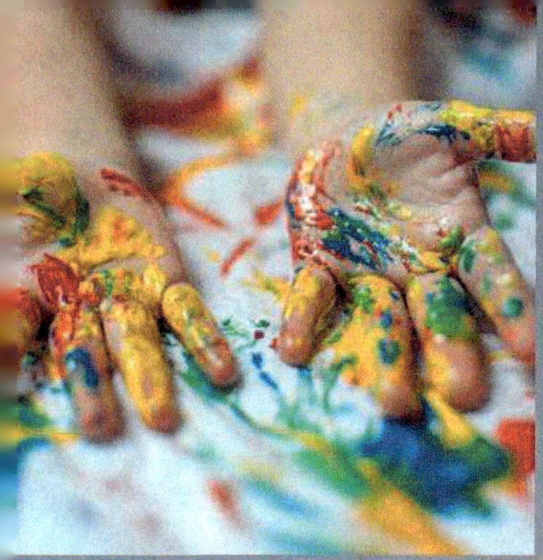
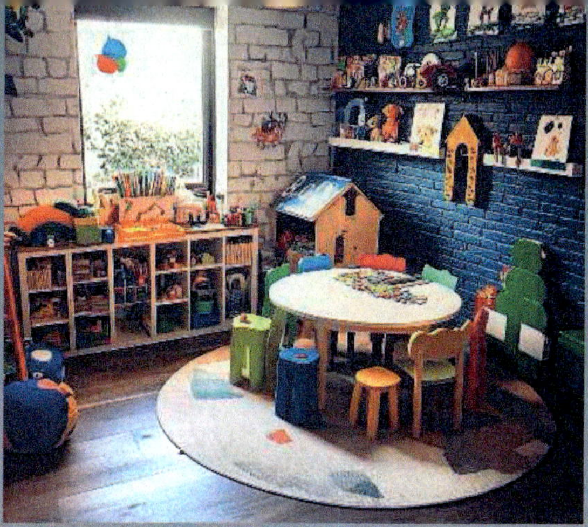
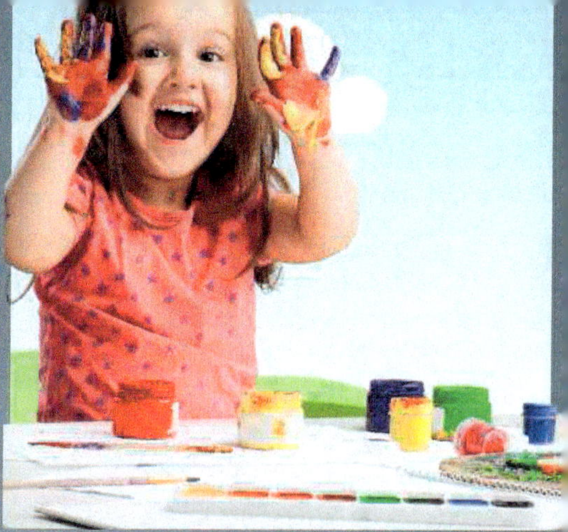
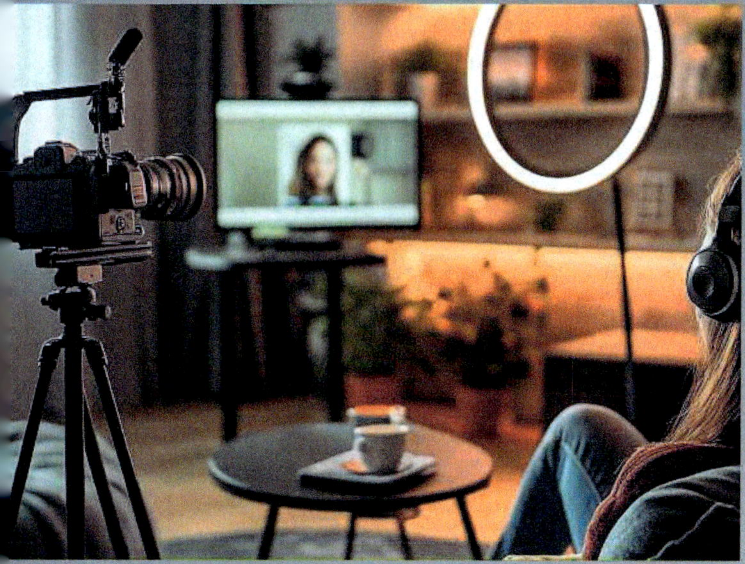
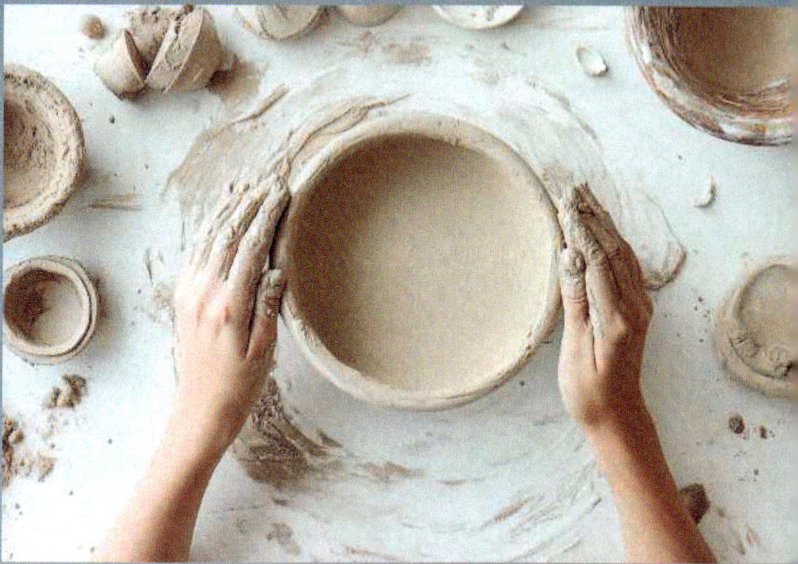
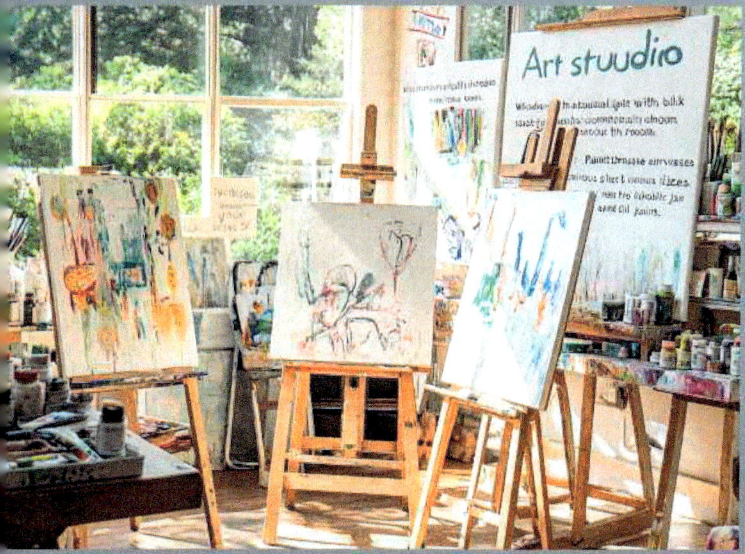
Art stuudio
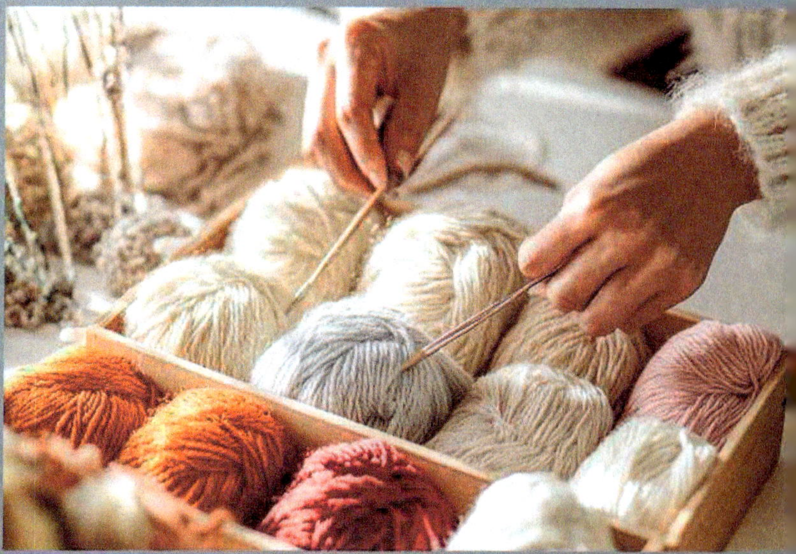
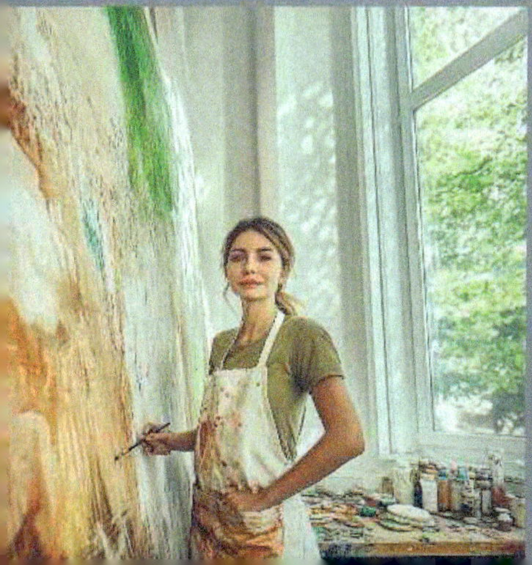
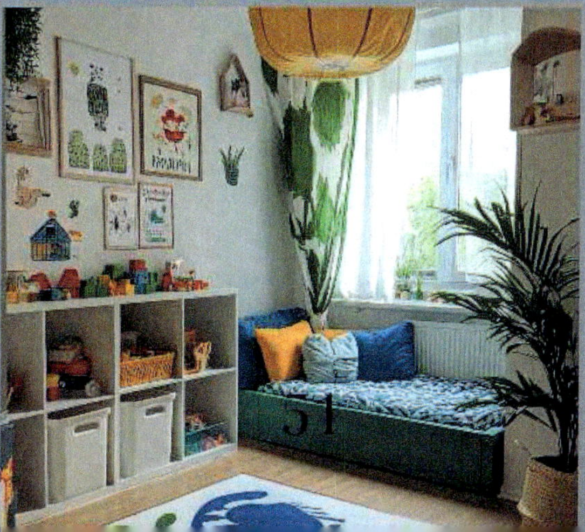
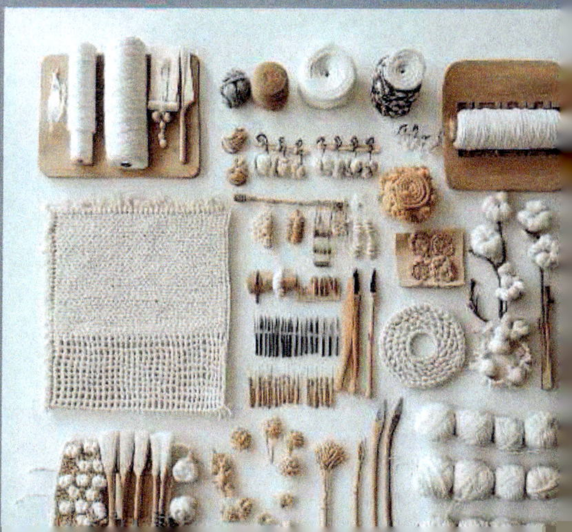

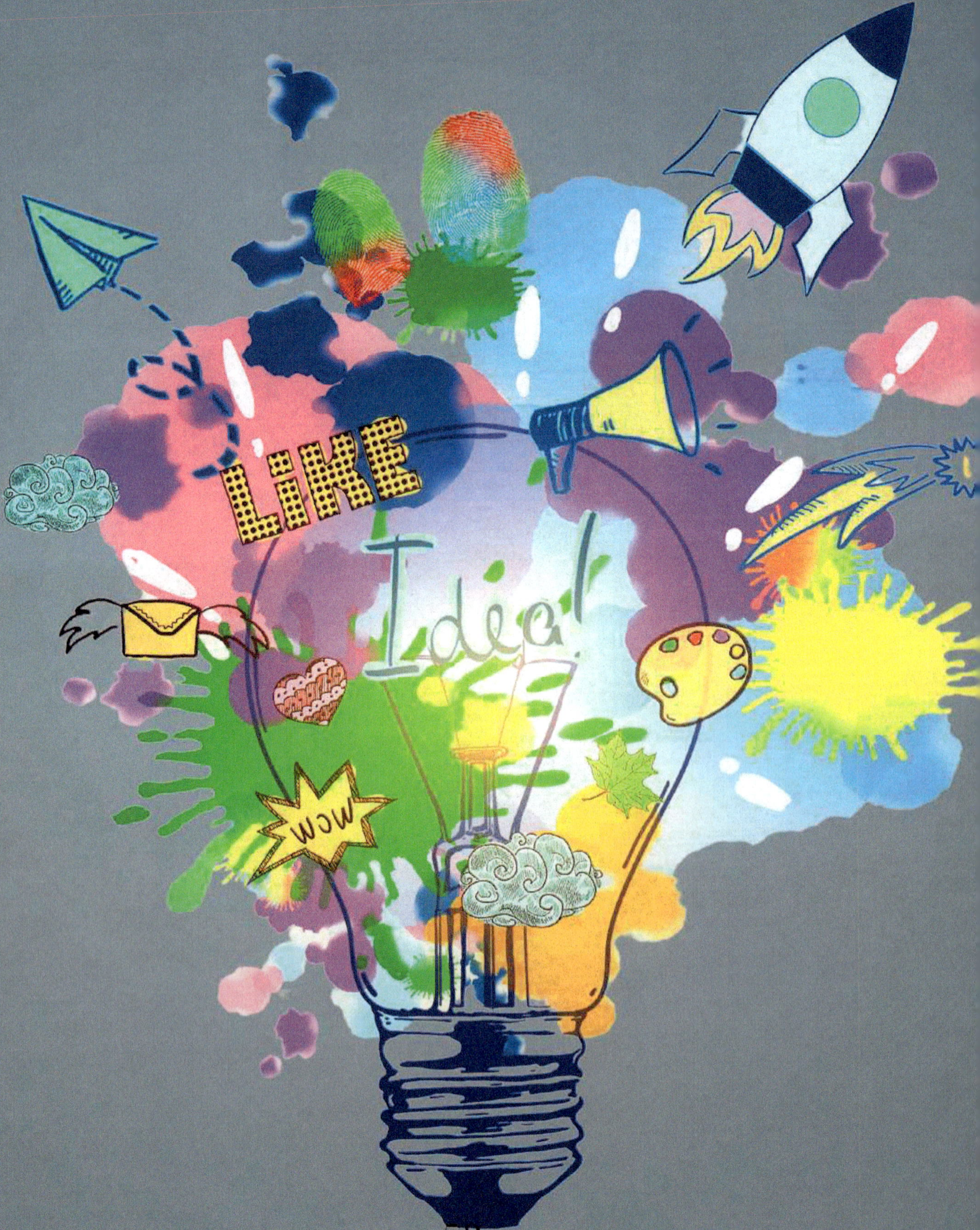
LIKE
Idea!
WOW

Unleash your inner child — That's where the genius lives

Grow wild. Think big. Make beautiful messes

The greatest inventions begin with 'What if?'

The more you play, the more you create. The more you create, the more you shine

Don't just teach creativity — protect it, celebrate it, set it free

Tiny hands can build giant dreams

Every masterpiece begins with a blank page and an open heart

Your uniqueness is your superpower. Create like No one else can

Art isn't a subject — it's a superpowe

The world needs more crayon-colored dreams and finger-painted hope

Imagination is the first language of the soul

Create with the freedom of a child and the wonder of a dreamer.

Magic begins the moment a child believes their art matters

Messy hands. Wild hearts. Masterpieces in the making

In every child lives a universe of colors waiting to be set free

Let their dreams be louder than rules, and their colors bolder than fear.

KNOWLEDGE & GROWTH

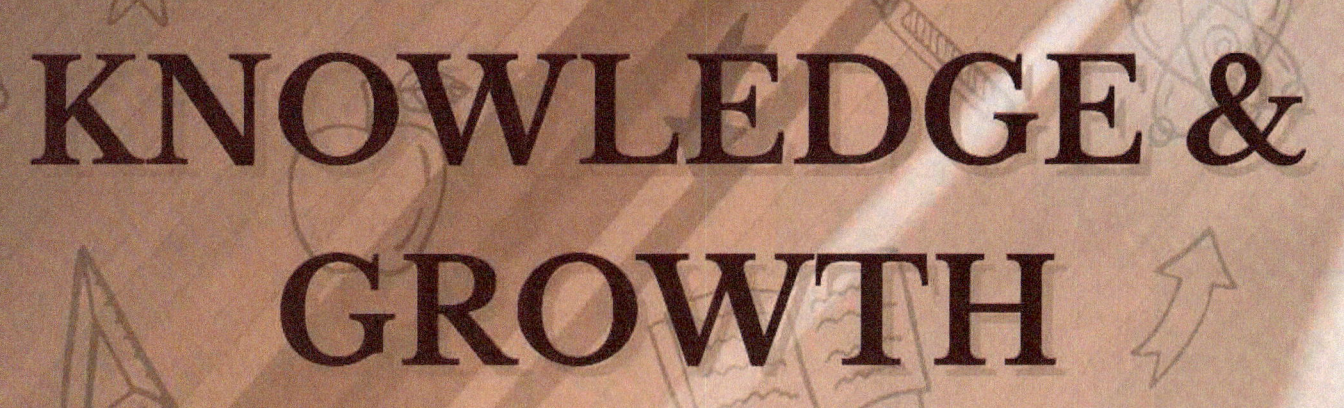

IN THE QUIET PURSUIT OF KNOWLEDGE, WE GROW BEYOND WHO WE WERE

VISUALIZE YOUR PATH TO GROWTH

Motivational Quote
"Through creativity, children speak the language of their soul."

How to Use This Section
Visualize the person you're becoming.
Is it the one who reads before bed, signs up for that course, or finally speaks up in the meeting? Growth doesn't happen all at once — it happens in every book opened, every new idea explored, every skill practiced.

Use this section to dream boldly, invest in your mind, and honor your evolution.

Affirmations to Inspire:
– *"I am committed to lifelong learning."*
– *"Every day, I expand my mind and strengthen my spirit."*
– *"Growth begins with one brave question."*
– *"My knowledge is my power."*
– *"I welcome change because I trust my growth."*

Inspiring Images to Include
- Open book with handwritten notes
- Online course on a laptop with a cup of tea
- Bookshelf filled with inspiring titles
- Notebooks, highlighters, planner on a tidy desk
- Peaceful study nook with sunlight and greenery
- Graduation cap, certificate, or library card
- Woman writing in a journal or reading by candlelight

Visualization Practice: Step into Your Wisdom
Take a deep breath.
Picture a warm space where joy lives — a table filled with color, your child's laughter echoing through the room, tiny hands discovering the world through color, shape, and sound.
You're not just raising a child — you're raising a thinker, a feeler, a creator.
See their eyes light up with pride as they show you what they made.
And remember: in every moment of play, a dream is forming.

Growth Habits to Manifest
- Read daily — even a page is progress
- Ask more questions
- Write your thoughts down — they matter
- Watch something that teaches, not just entertains
- Celebrate progress, not perfection

ONLINE CLASSES

> "AN INVESTMENT IN KNOWLEDGE ALWAYS PAYS THE BEST INTEREST."
> *Benjamin Franklin*

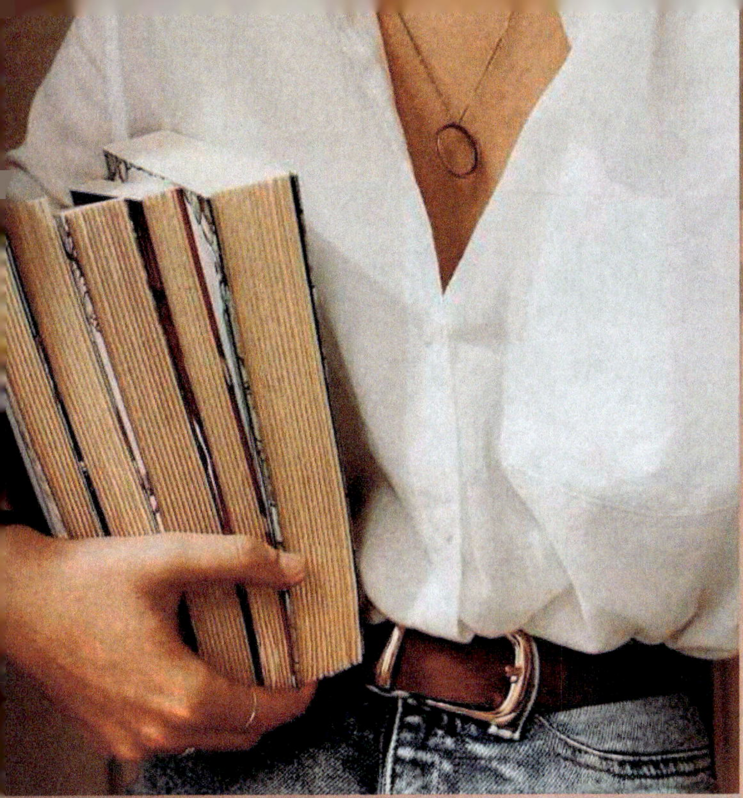
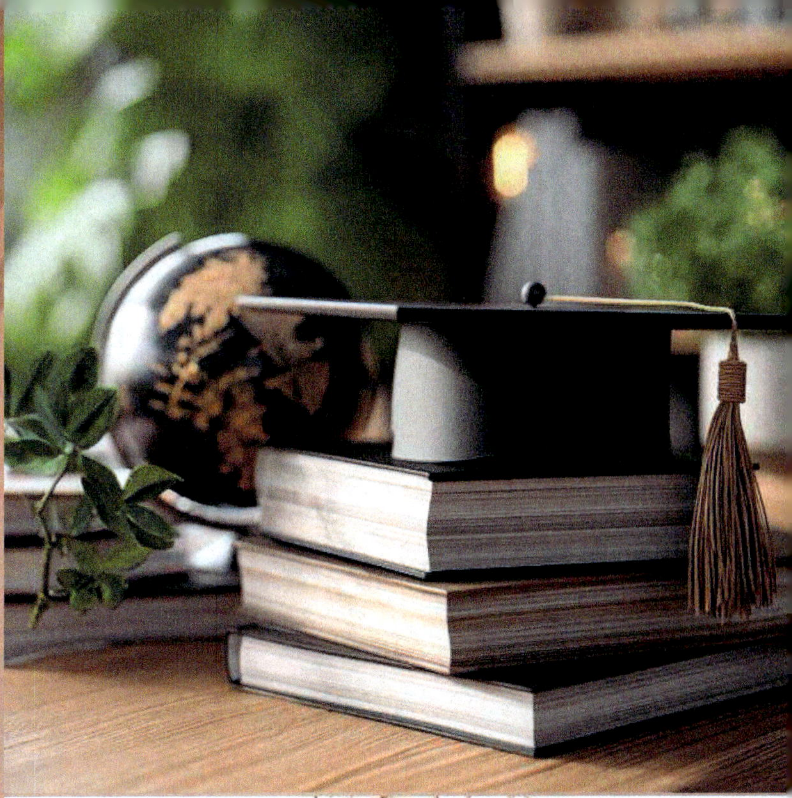
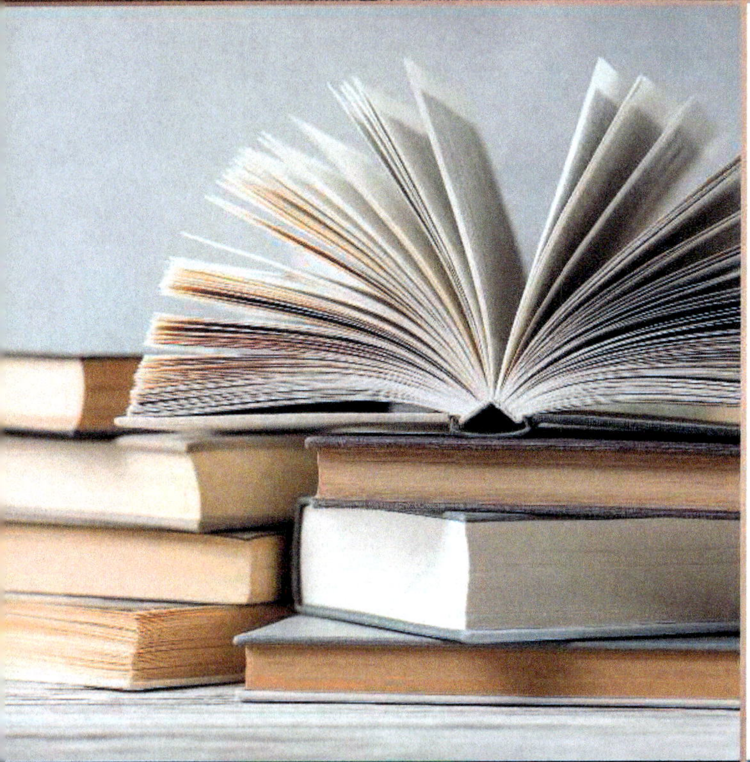
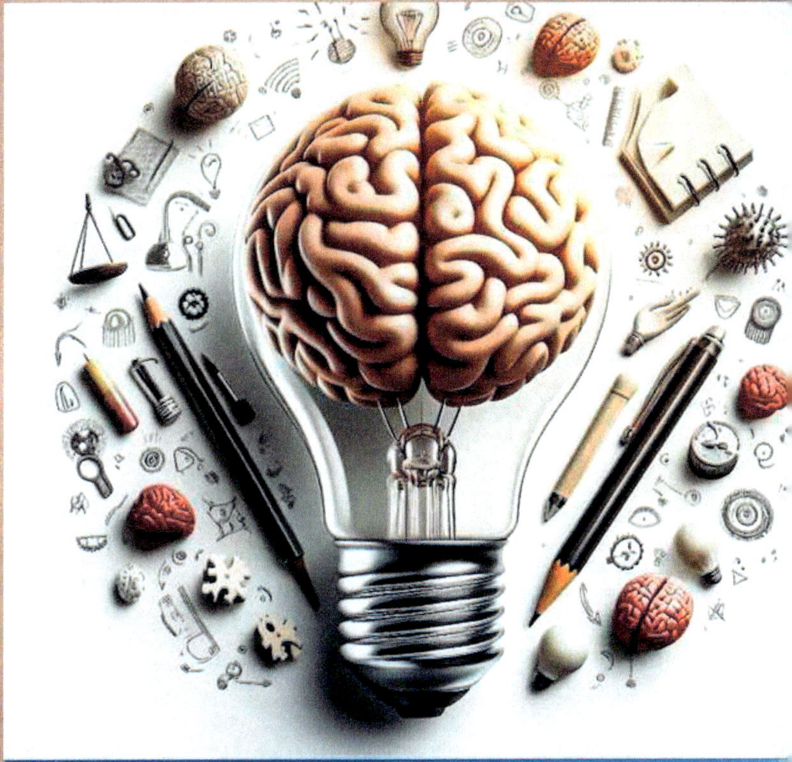
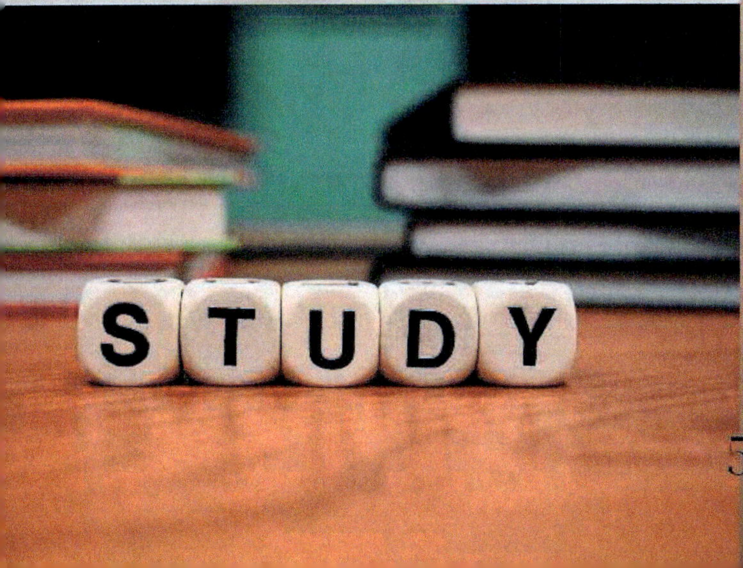
STUDY
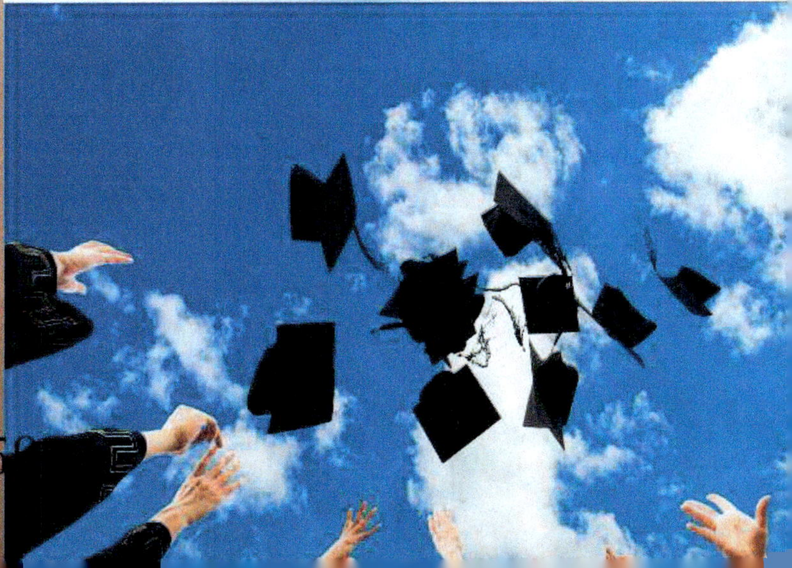

"Feed your brain like you feed your soul — daily, gently, intentionally

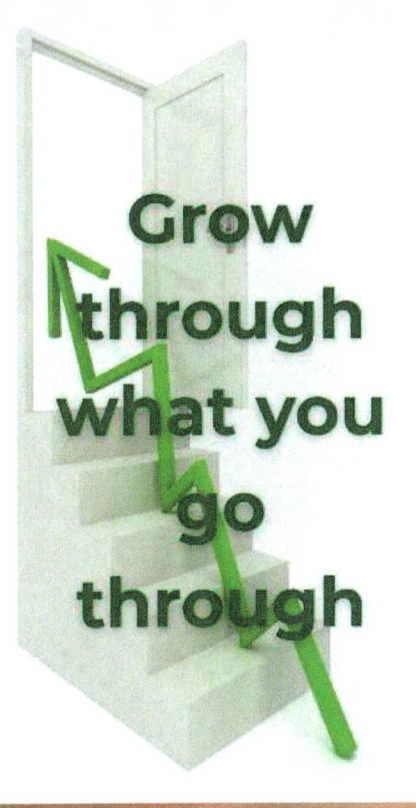

- Grow through what you go through
- Learn something new every day. Your future self will thank you 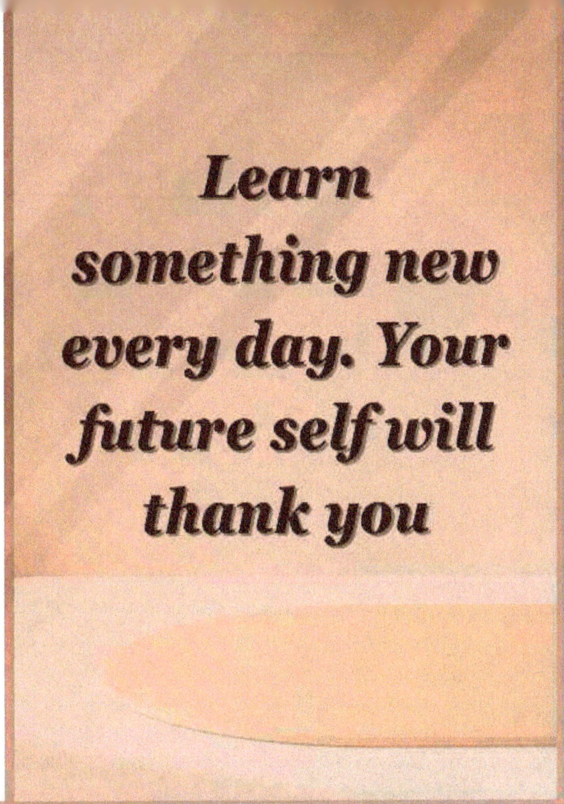
- Knowledge is your power. Use it to build your world 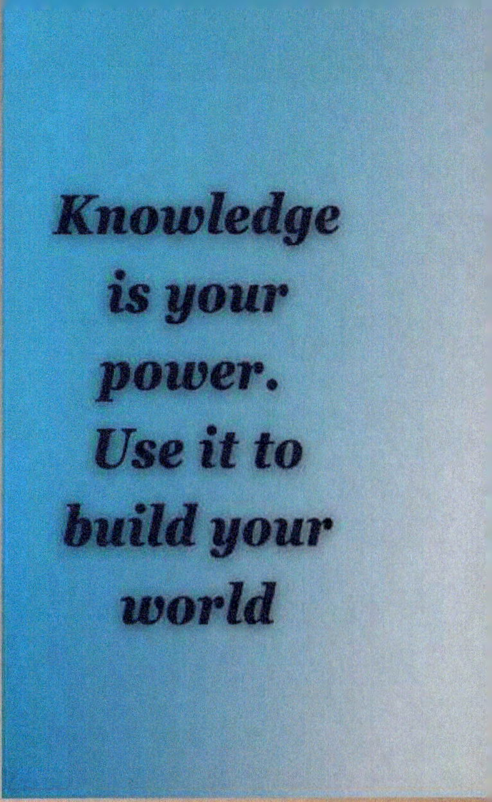
- Dream. Learn. Evolve. Repeat 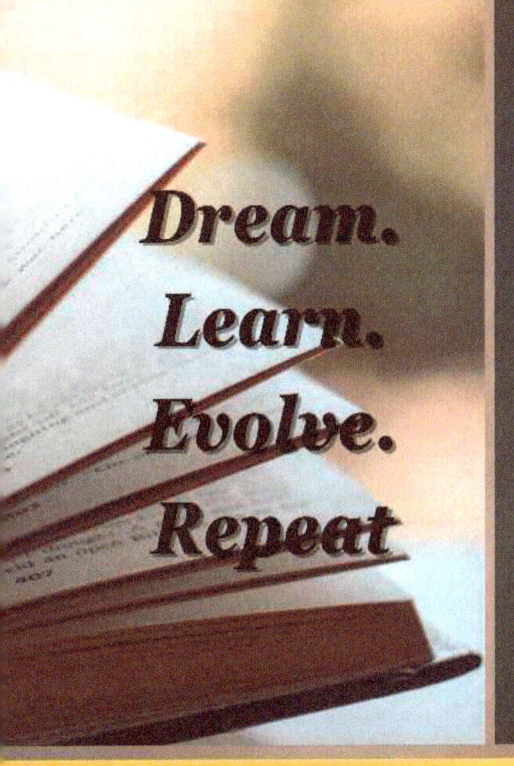
- Study your passion like it's your mission 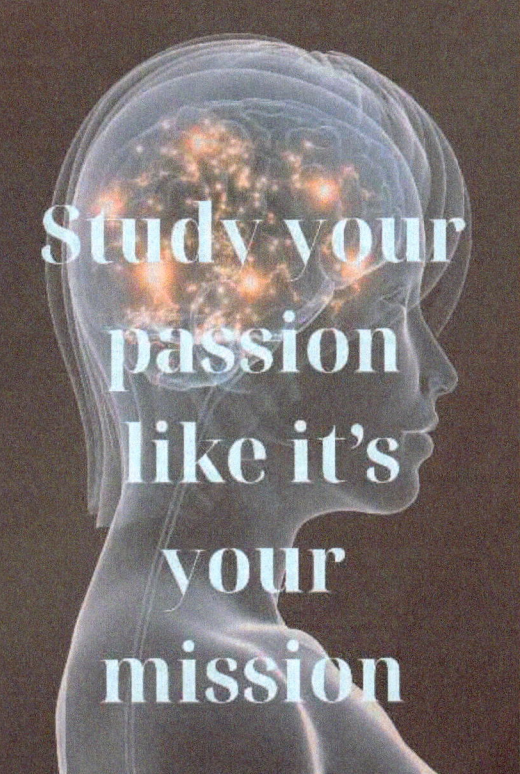
- Your mind is your greatest investment 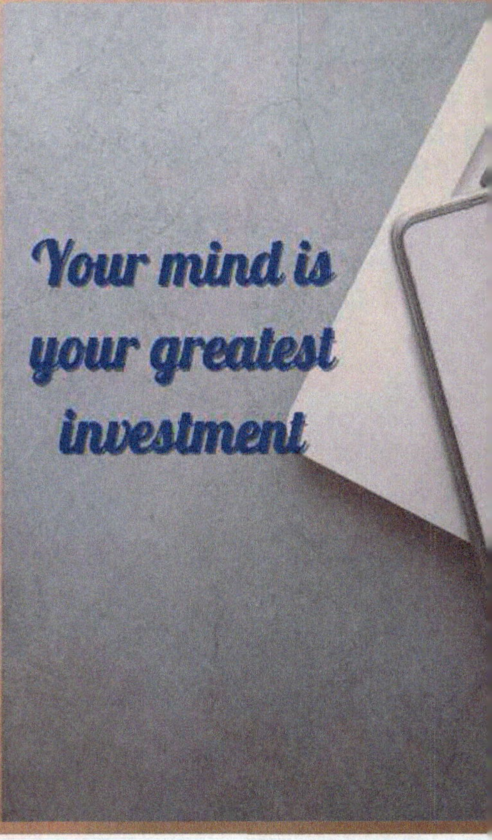
- Expand your knowledge, expand your life 
- There is beauty in becoming — never rush the growth

Read. Reflect. Rise	Creativity It's not a talent — it's your soul speaking out loud	Stay curious. Stay open. Stay evolving
Your potential is limitless when you choose to grow	Build your mind like you build your empire — brick by brick	She's not chasing trends — she's chasing growth
Books are portals. Open one and enter a new version of yourself		Small steps every day create powerful transformations

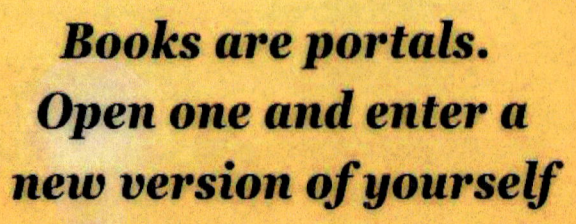

CAREER & WORK

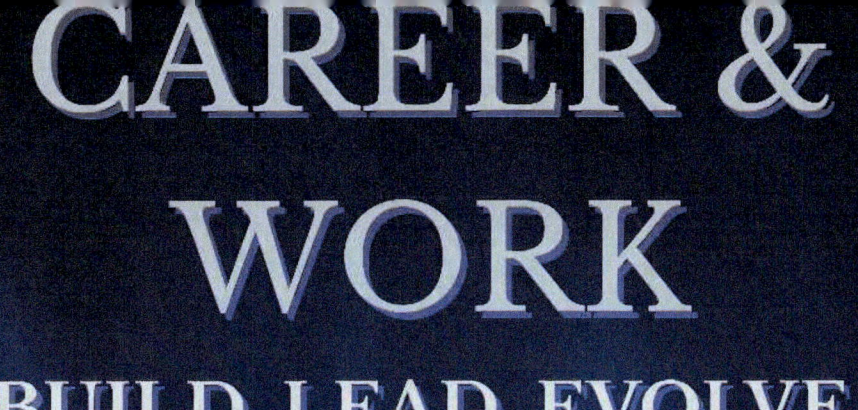

BUILD. LEAD. EVOLVE.

VISUALIZE YOUR CAREER SUCCESS

MOTIVATIONAL QUOTE:
"Your career is not just a job — it's your impact in action."

HOW TO USE THIS SECTION
Visualize the professional life that excites and fulfills you.
Are you building your own business, stepping into leadership, or finally doing work that reflects your true self?
This section is your space to dream boldly about the work you were born to do.

Think of your goals not just as titles or salaries, but as the legacy you're creating through your effort, vision, and passion.

AFFIRMATIONS FOR AMBITION
– *"I am building a career I love and believe in."*
– *"Every step I take brings me closer to my professional purpose."*
– *"Opportunities flow to me because I am ready."*
– *"I lead with vision, passion, and clarity."*
– *"Success is not a destination — it's how I show up daily."*

INSPIRING IMAGES TO INCLUDE
A sleek office setup or modern workspace
A woman giving a powerful presentation or leading a meeting
Calendar with big goals marked and deadlines met
Stylish desk with laptop, coffee, and vision board
Closed deals, signed contracts, or creative brainstorming sessions
A CEO nameplate, business card mockup, or brand logo
Elevator buttons lit up, symbolizing career elevation

PRO CAREER HABITS TO MANIFEST:
Write down your wins — even small ones
• Speak up when your ideas matter
• Build connections — collaboration fuels growth
• Invest in learning new skills
• Show up like the person who already has the job

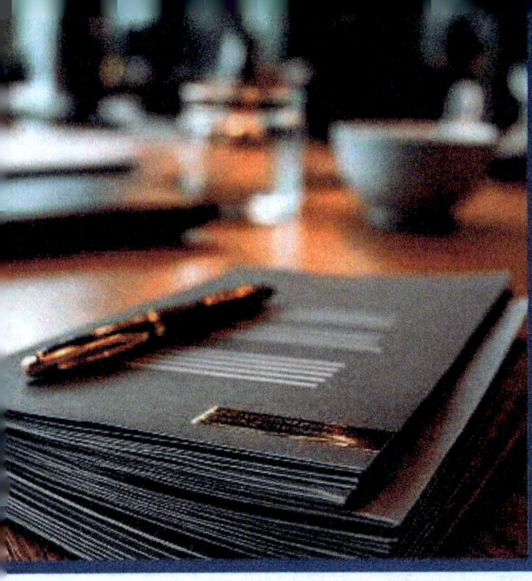

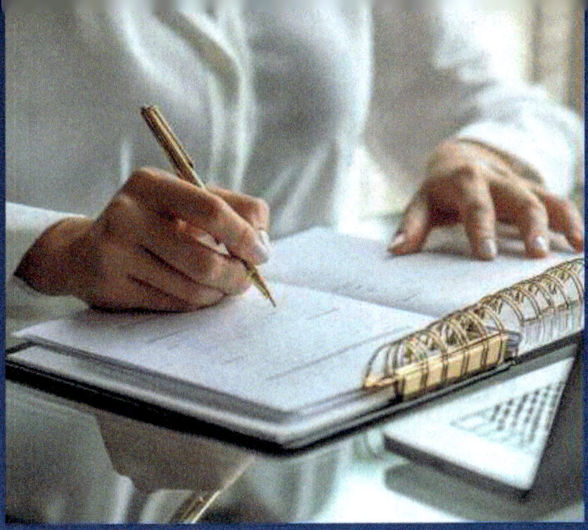

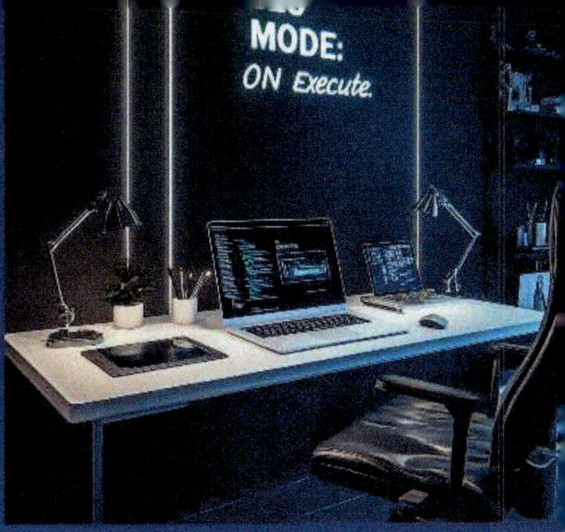
MODE:
ON Execute.

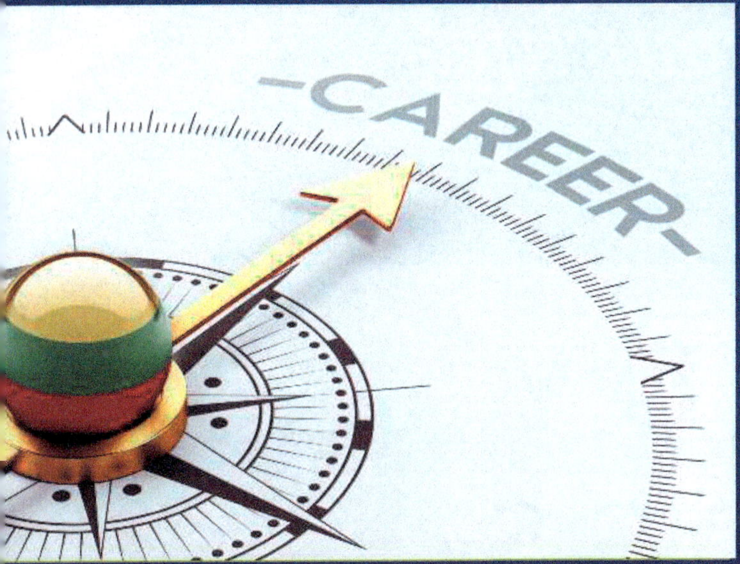
-CAREER-

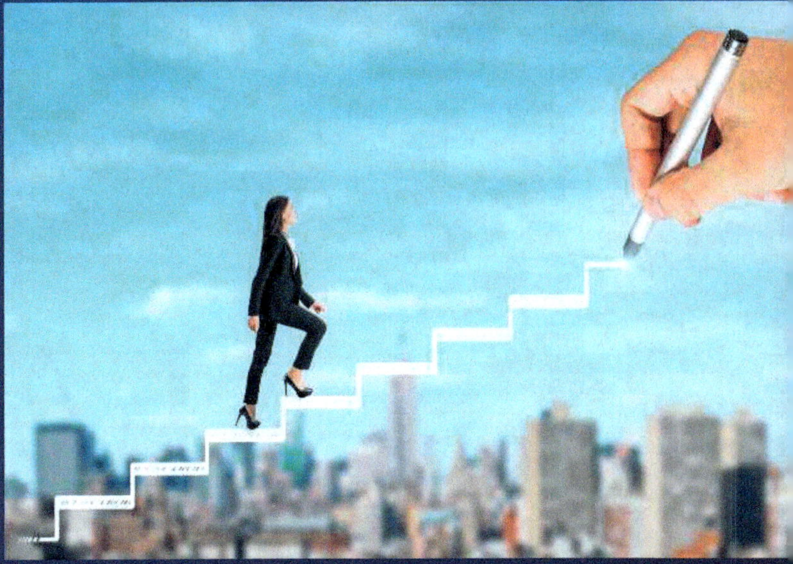

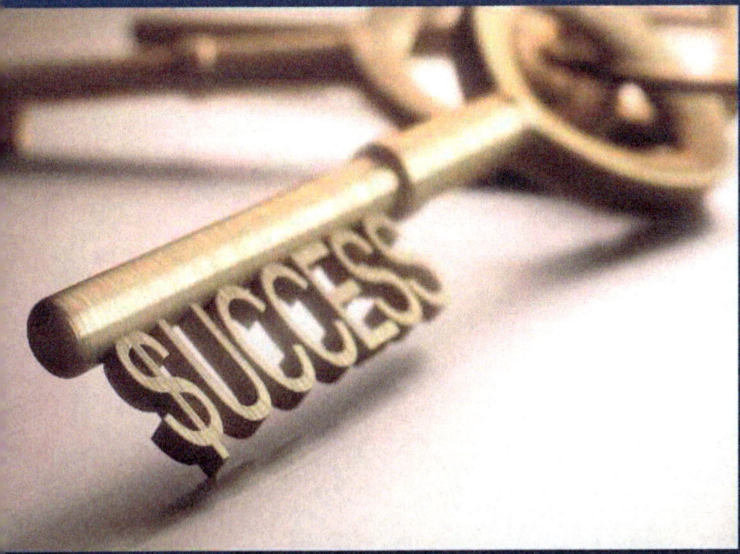
SUCCESS

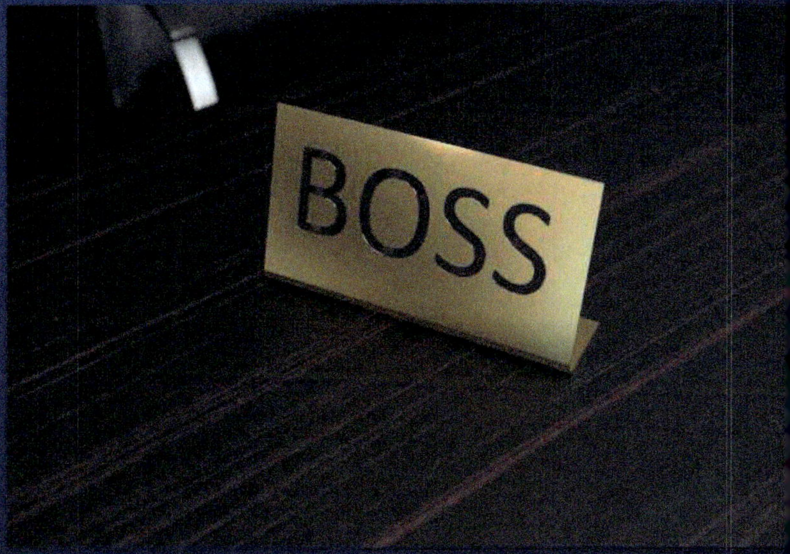
BOSS

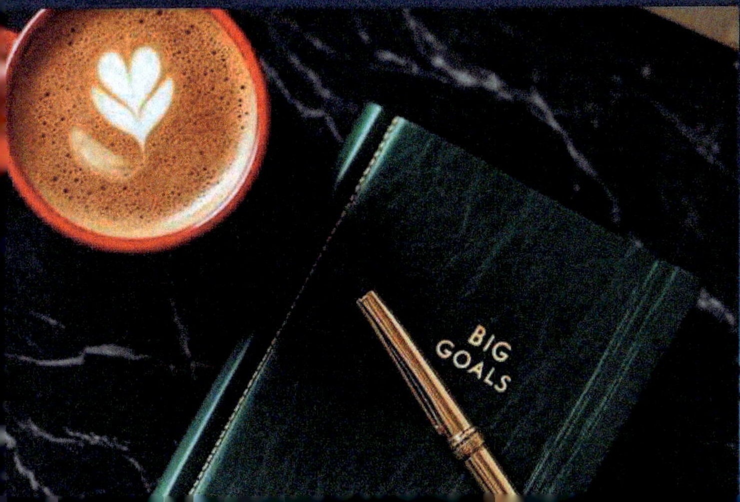
BIG
GOALS

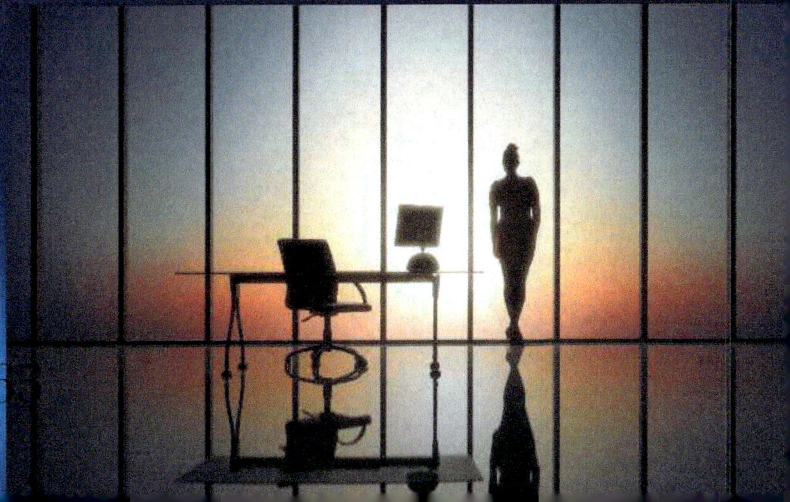

*"Choose a job you love,
and you will never have to work
a day in your life."*
Confucius

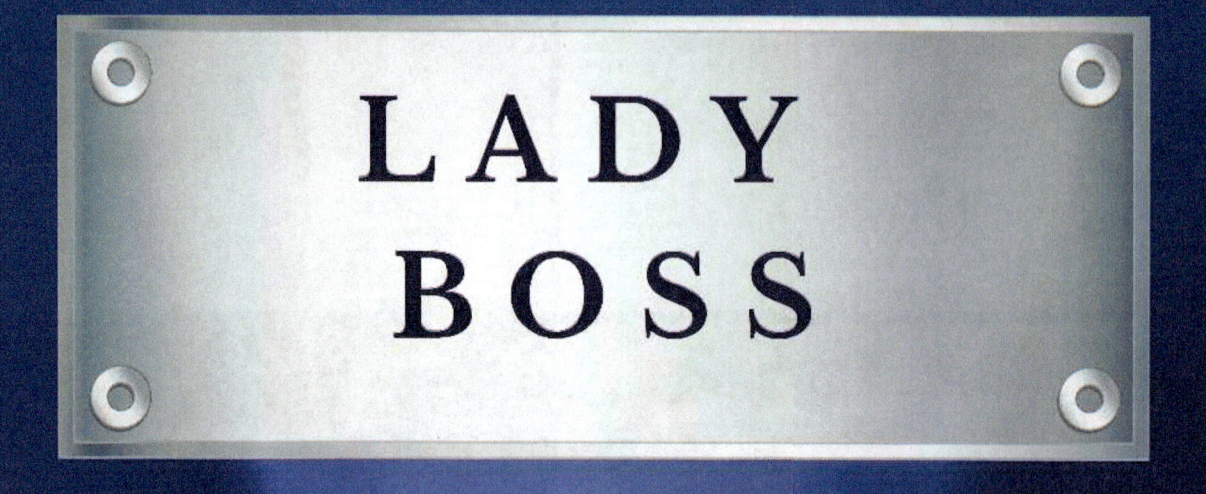

LADY BOSS

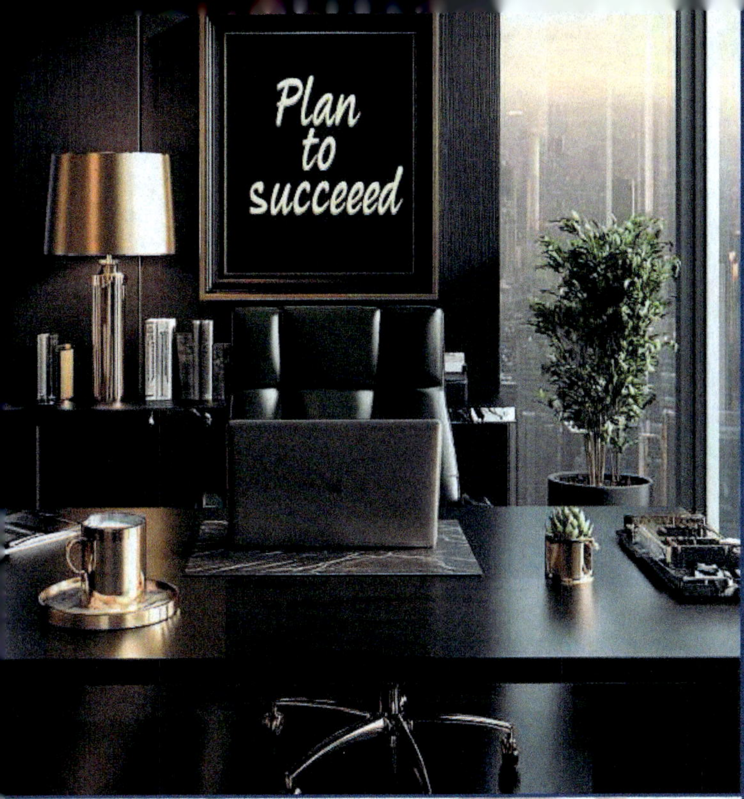
Plan
to
succeeed
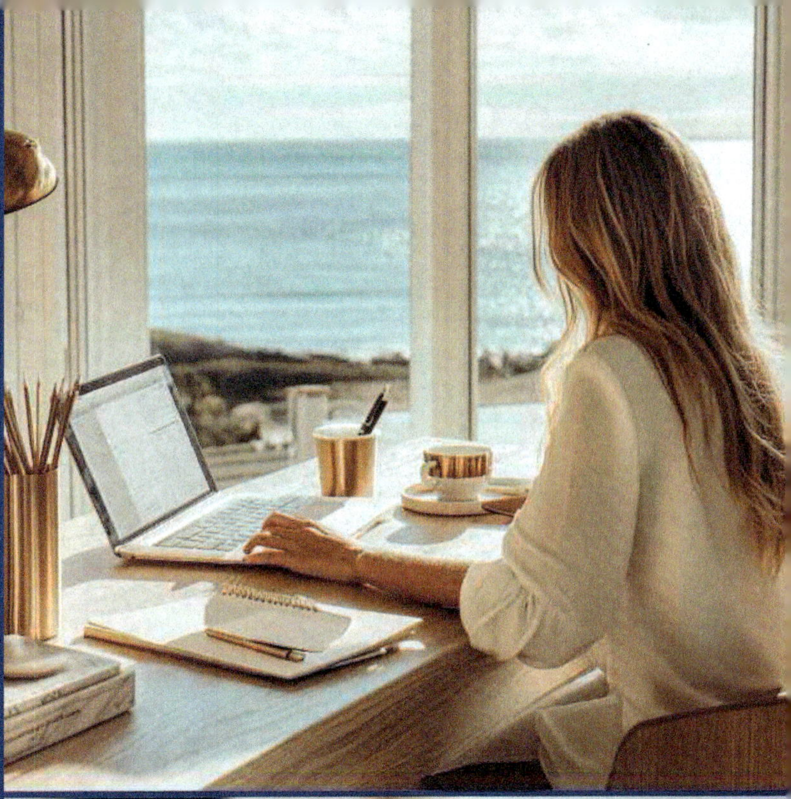
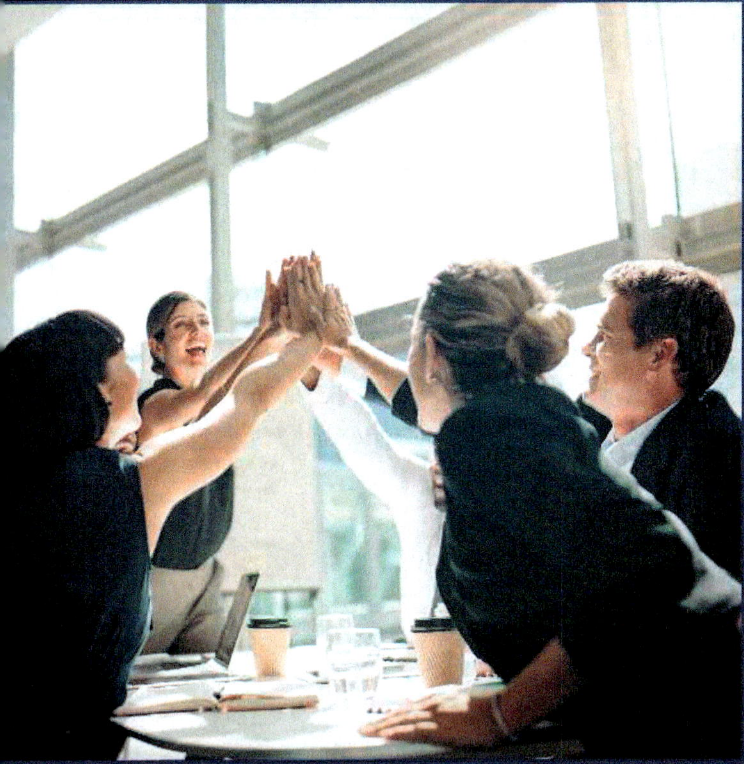
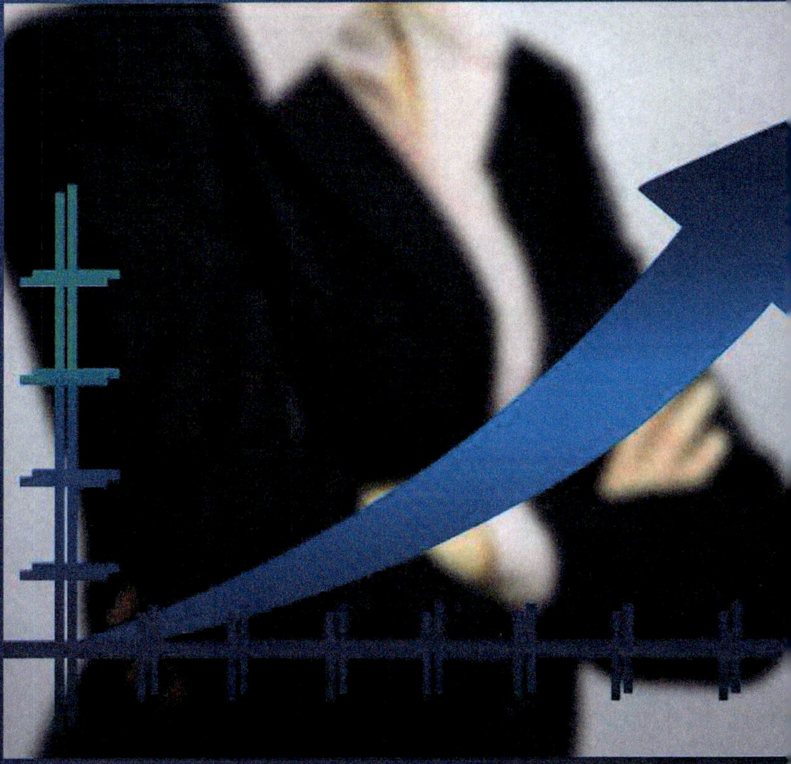
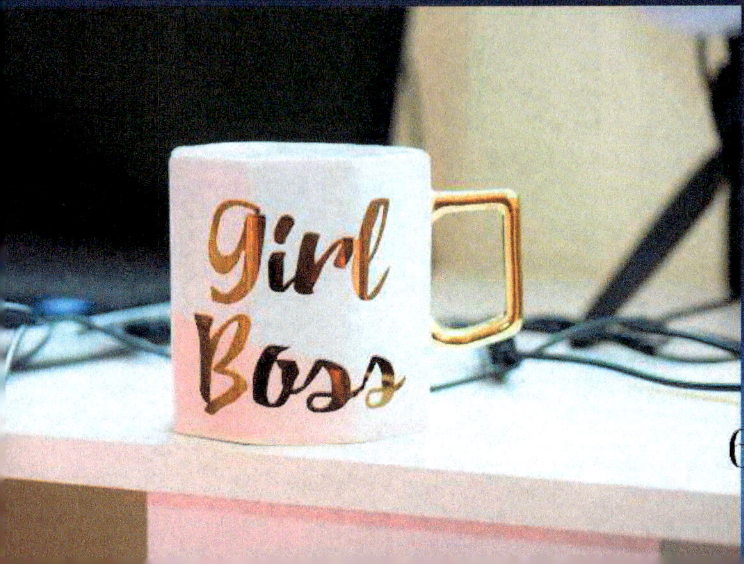
Girl
Boss
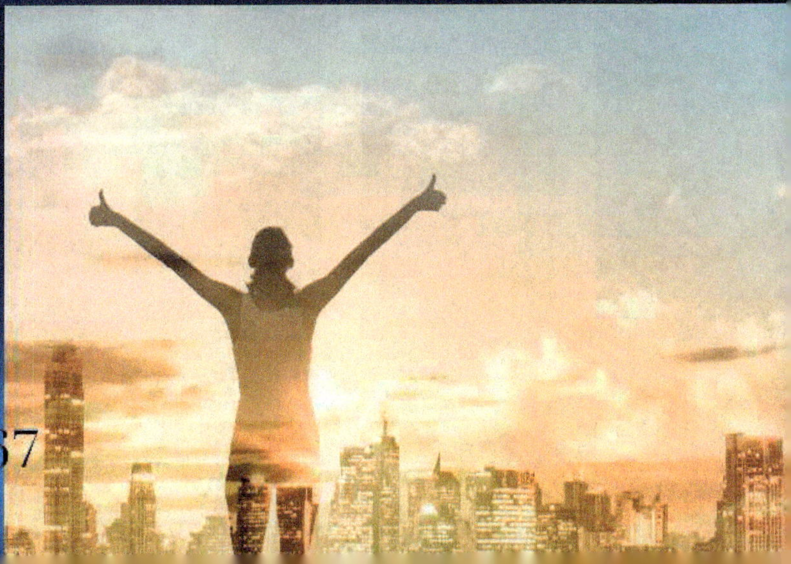

CAREER

ACT

GROW

LEAD

THRIVE

Your dream job doesn't exist — you must create it

Success loves the relentless

Today's grind is tomorrow's greatness

Turn passion into power and power into progress

Be the *CEO* of your destiny.

Stay professional. Stay hungry. Stay unstoppable

The hustle is temporary. The success is permanent

Opportunities don't just happen — you create them with courage.

Turn your ambition into your paycheck	Ambition is the first step to success. Action is the second	Work until your signature becomes an autograph
Build a career you can't wait to wake up to	Your career is your empire. Build it brick by brick	Work silently. Let your success make the noise.
When you work for your dreams, your dreams work for you		Focus on your goal. Glow through your hustle.

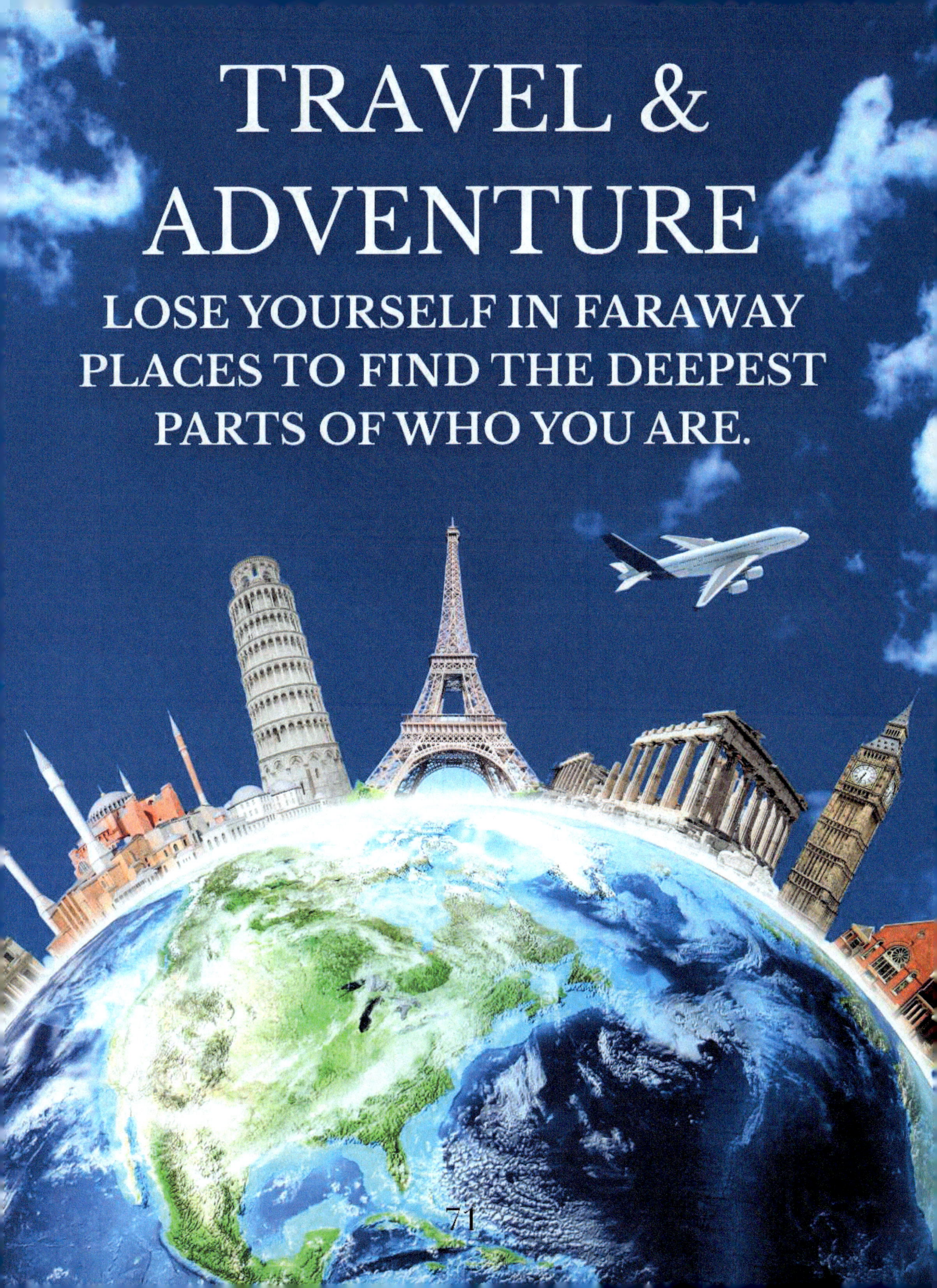

TRAVEL & ADVENTURE

LOSE YOURSELF IN FARAWAY PLACES TO FIND THE DEEPEST PARTS OF WHO YOU ARE.

VISUALIZE YOUR JOURNEY OF TRAVEL & ADVENTURE

MOTIVATIONAL QUOTE:

"Lose yourself in faraway places to find the deepest parts of who you are."

HOW TO USE THIS SECTION

Choose images that inspire a sense of adventure:
Breathtaking landscapes
Open roads and endless skies
Passports, luggage, and travel essentials
Moments of freedom and exploration

CREATE ADVENTURE AFFIRMATIONS

Add phrases like:
"I am open to new adventures."
"The world welcomes me with wonder and excitement."
"Every journey enriches my soul."
"Adventure flows effortlessly into my life."

SET YOUR TRAVEL GOALS. WRITE YOUR 1-YEAR MILESTONES:

Plan a dream trip
Explore a new country or city
Embrace spontaneous adventures
Capture memories that will last a lifetime

VISUALIZATION PRACTICE

Manifest Your Next Adventure:
Take 5 minutes to close your eyes.
Picture yourself walking new streets, seeing new sights, feeling the thrill of the unknown.
Engage your senses: the scent of the ocean, the taste of exotic food, the sound of new languages.
Smile. Your next great adventure is already on its way.

ACTIONABLE ADVENTURE TIPS

Say yes to opportunities for travel and exploration, big or small.
Step outside your comfort zone to experience the magic of the unfamiliar.
Document your journeys — your story is a treasure.
Trust your instincts and let your heart guide your path.

"Adventure Awaits..."

73

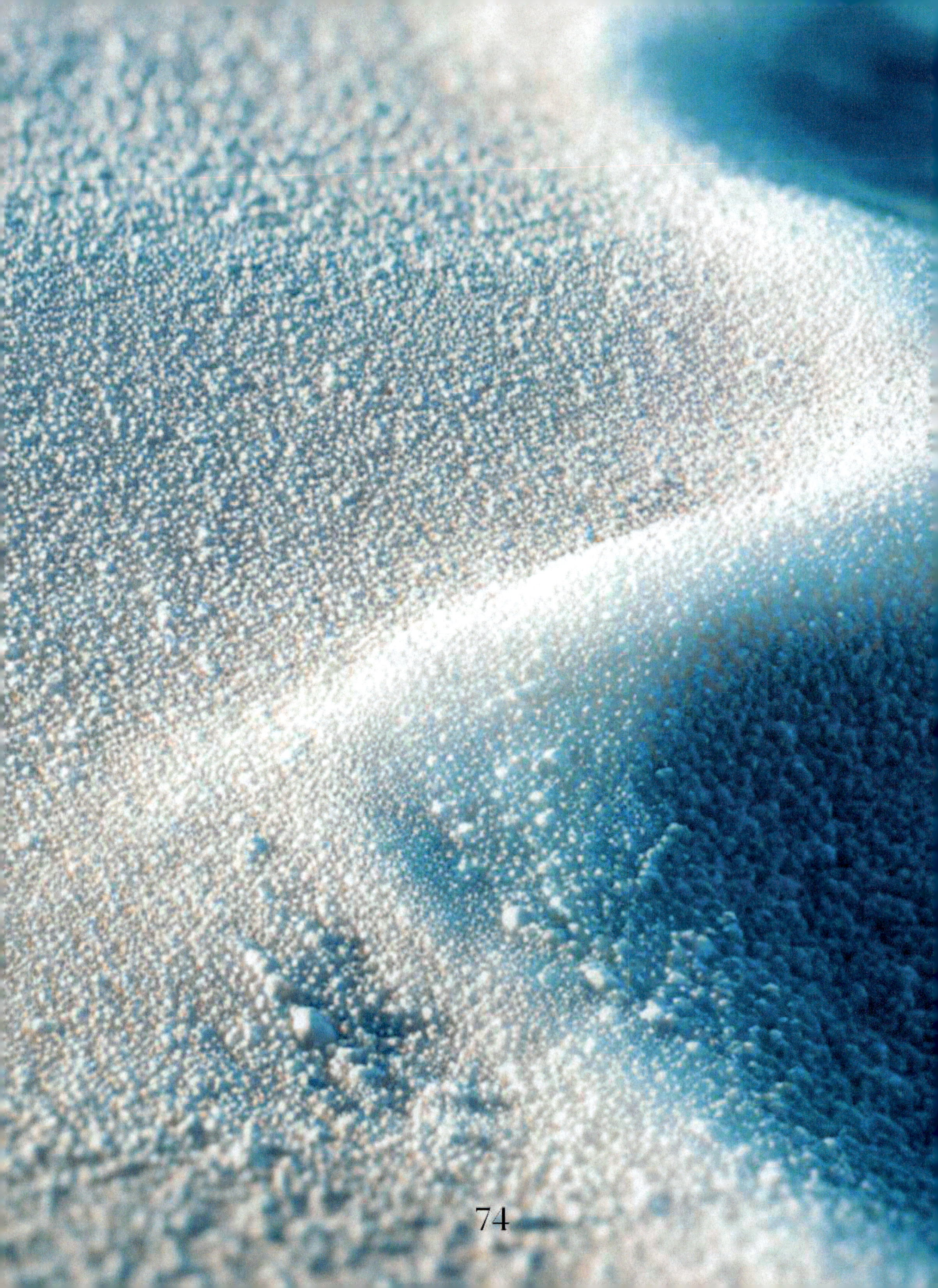

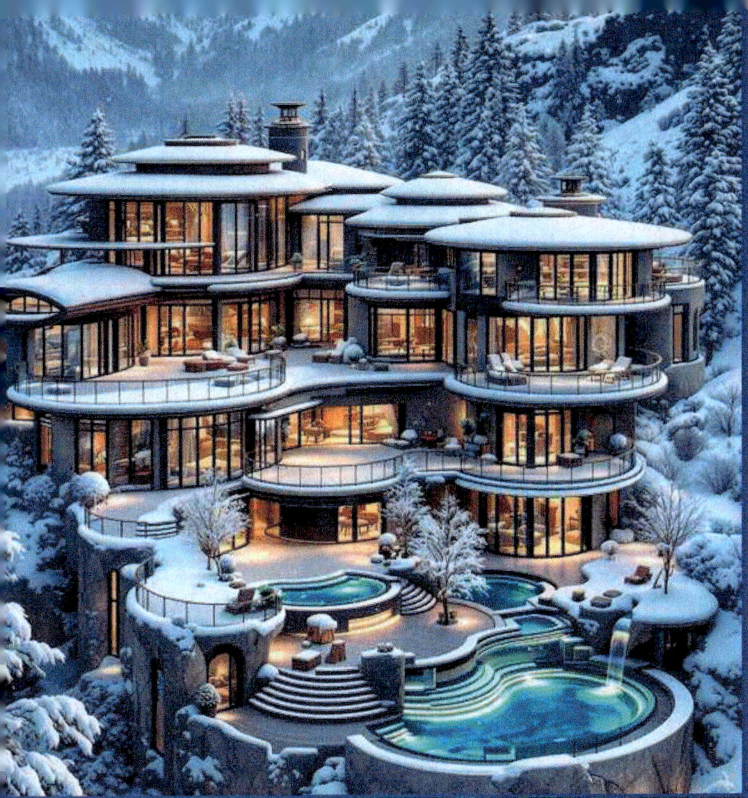
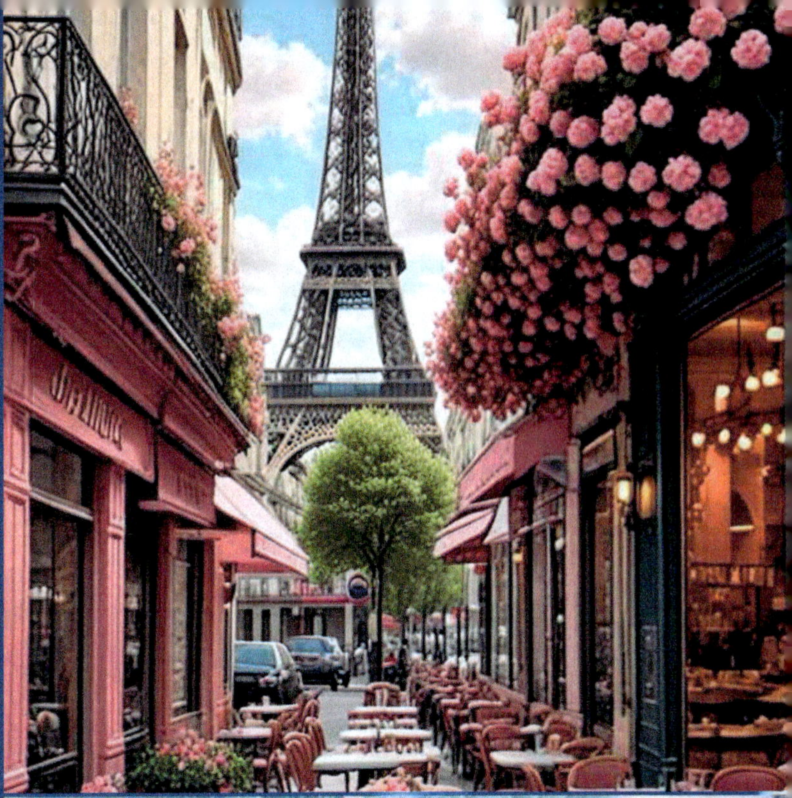
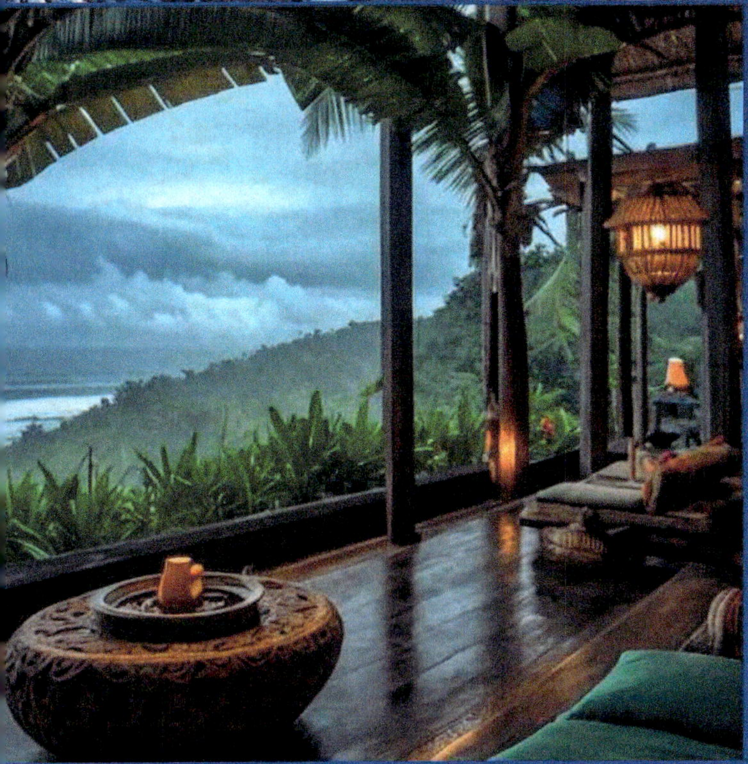
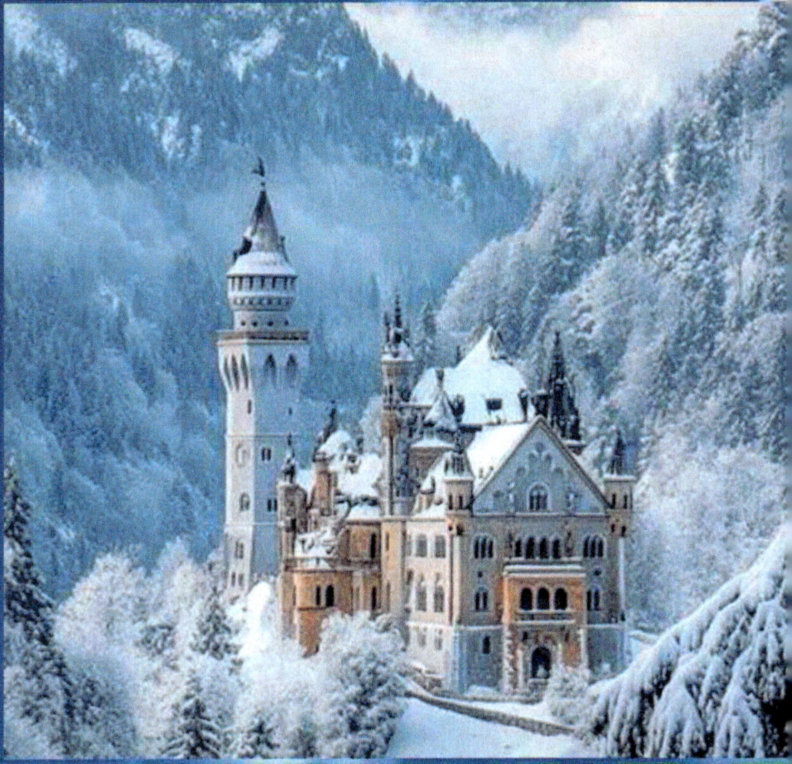
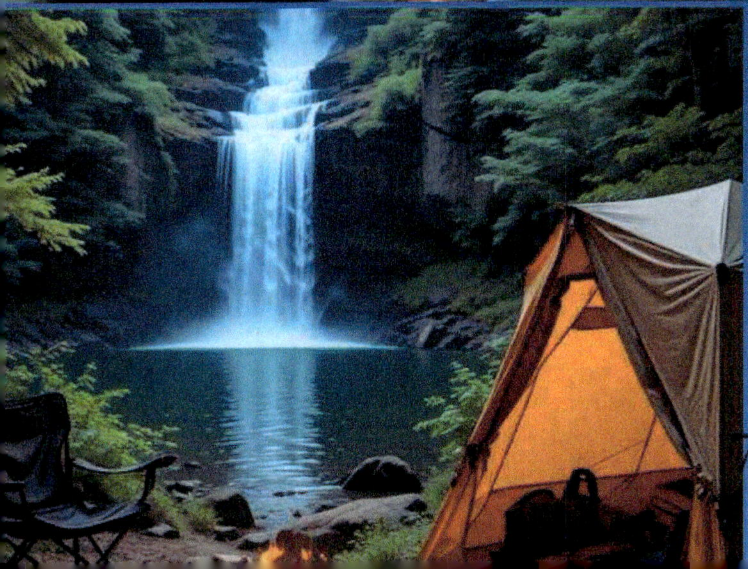
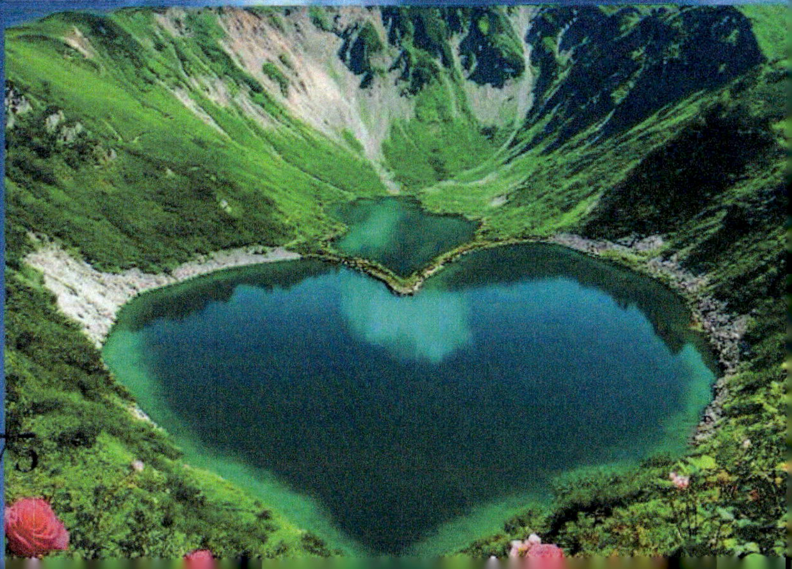

76

The world whispers in colors unknown — follow the call and paint your adventure

Carry the sun in your heart and let every journey begin with a spark of wonder

Between the earth and the sky lies the path of dreamers and explorers

Travel is a love letter you write to the world, one step at a time

Wander through the world with wide eyes and a wild soul

Chasing horizons, we find not just places, but ourselves

Every sunrise promises a new story. Every journey writes a new chapter

Let the winds of adventure carry your soul across endless skies

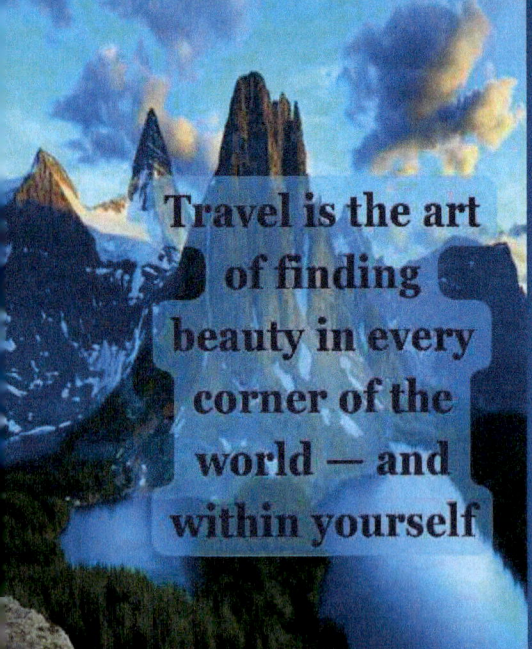

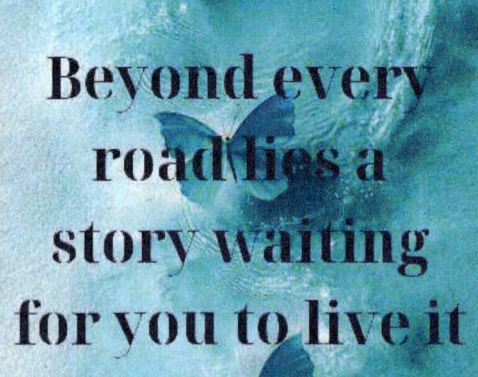

Adventure is not found on the map — it's woven into the steps of the brave

Where your dreams meet distant lands — there begins the true adventure

In every journey, you find pieces of the magic you were always meant to chase

Travel is the art of finding beauty in every corner of the world — and within yourself

Beyond every road lies a story waiting for you to live it

Set your spirit free – the world is your canvas, and adventure is your brush

Adventure awaits beyond every horizon

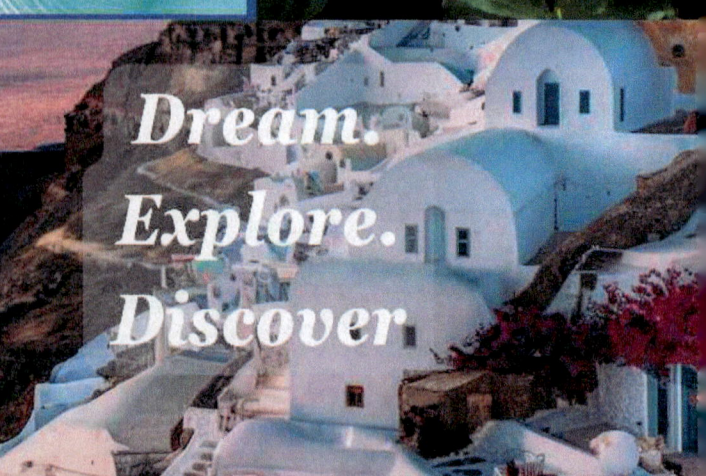

Dream. Explore. Discover

Choose Your Words of Power

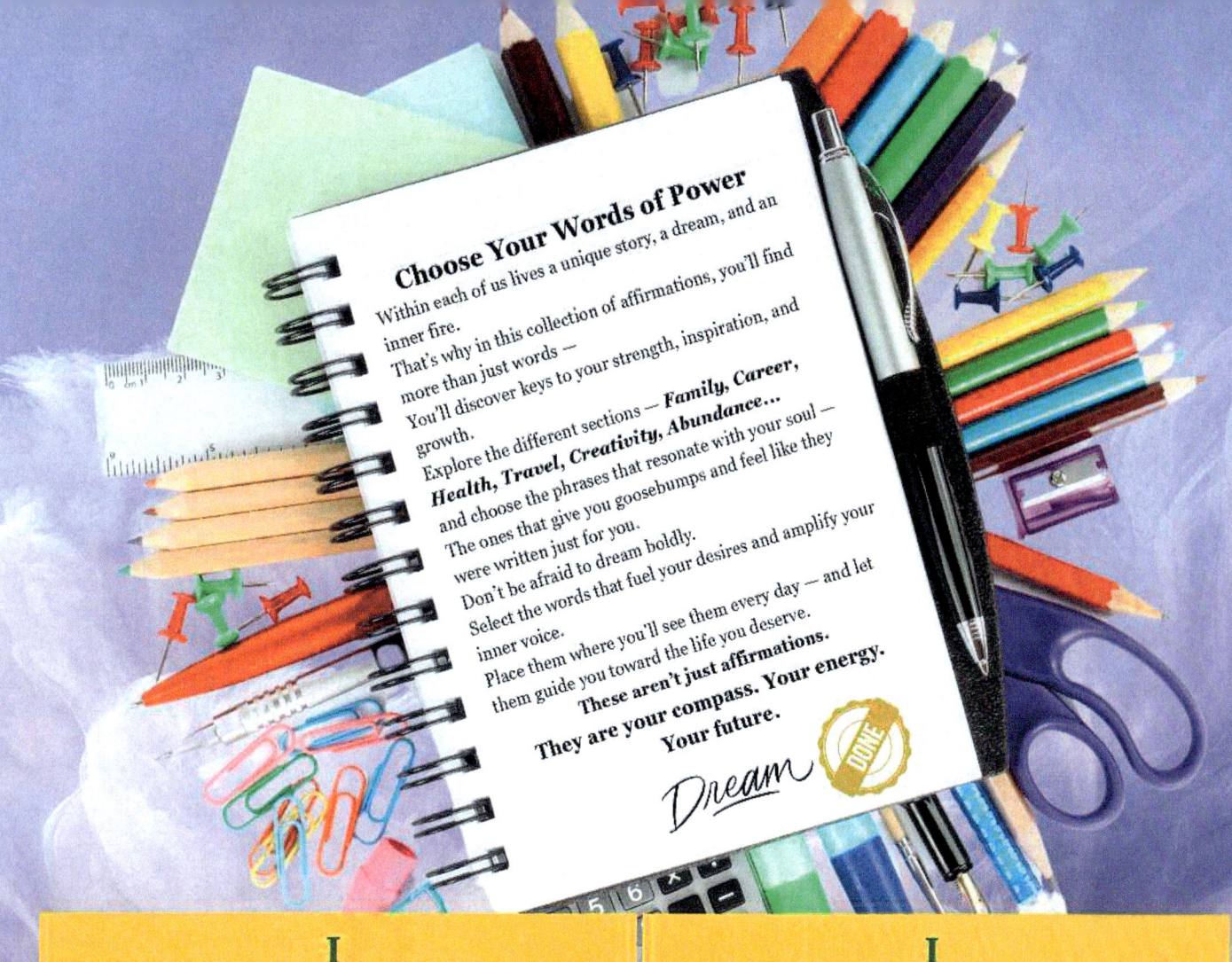

Within each of us lives a unique story, a dream, and an inner fire.

That's why in this collection of affirmations, you'll find more than just words —

You'll discover keys to your strength, inspiration, and growth.

Explore the different sections — **Family, Career, Health, Travel, Creativity, Abundance...** — and choose the phrases that resonate with your soul —

The ones that give you goosebumps and feel like they were written just for you.

Don't be afraid to dream boldly.

Select the words that fuel your desires and amplify your inner voice.

Place them where you'll see them every day — and let them guide you toward the life you deserve.

These aren't just affirmations.

They are your compass. Your energy. Your future.

Dream

I CHOOSE THE ENERGY OF LIFE	I LIVE A HEALTHY AND ACTIVE LIFE

I GET ENERGY FROM EVERY DAY	I CHOOSE A HEALTHY LIFESTYLE EVERY DAY	I TAKE CARE OF MY HEALTH
I FEEL GRATEFUL FOR MY HEALTH	I HAVE CLEAN AND HEALTHY SKIN	I HAVE ME - AND THAT'S MY POWER
I AM GRATEFUL FOR MY HEALTH	I LET MY BODY RECOVER	I GET ENERGY FROM EACH NEW DAY

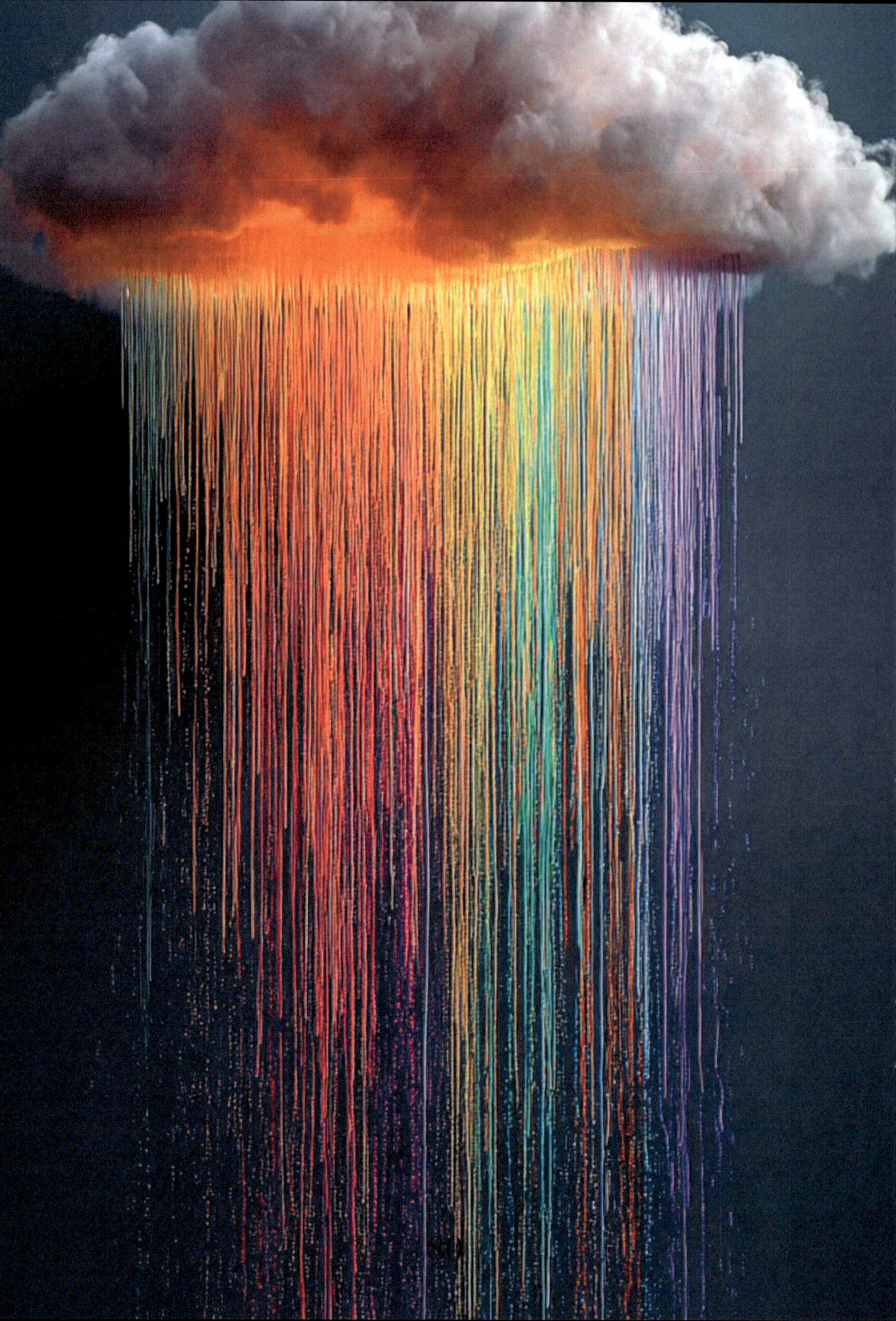

I EXPLORE THE WORLD		I CRAVE ADVENTURE
I FOLLOW THE SUN	I TRAVEL WITH PURPOSE	I COLLECT MEMORIES, NOT THINGS
I LIVE FOR NEW EXPERIENCES	I CHOOSE FREEDOM	I WANDER, I DISCOVER, I GROW
I TRAVEL EASILY AND ENJOY EVERY MOMENT	I PLAN MY TRIPS WITH INSPIRATION	I AM OPEN TO NEW ADVENTURES
I CHOOSE THE ENERGY OF LIFE		I WELCOME LOVE INTO MY LIFE
I OPEN MY HEART TO LOVE	**I LOVE!**	I LIVE IN HARMONY WITH MY BELOVED
I ATTRACT LOVE INTO MY LIFE	I ATTRACT A RELATIONSHIP THAT UPLIFTS AND INSPIRES ME	I FEEL HARMONY IN THE RELATIONSHIP I BUILD WITH MY PARTNER
I GIVE UNCONDITIONAL LOVE	I APPRECIATE EVERY MOMENT WITH MY BELOVED	I AM WORTHY OF LOVE AND AFFECTION

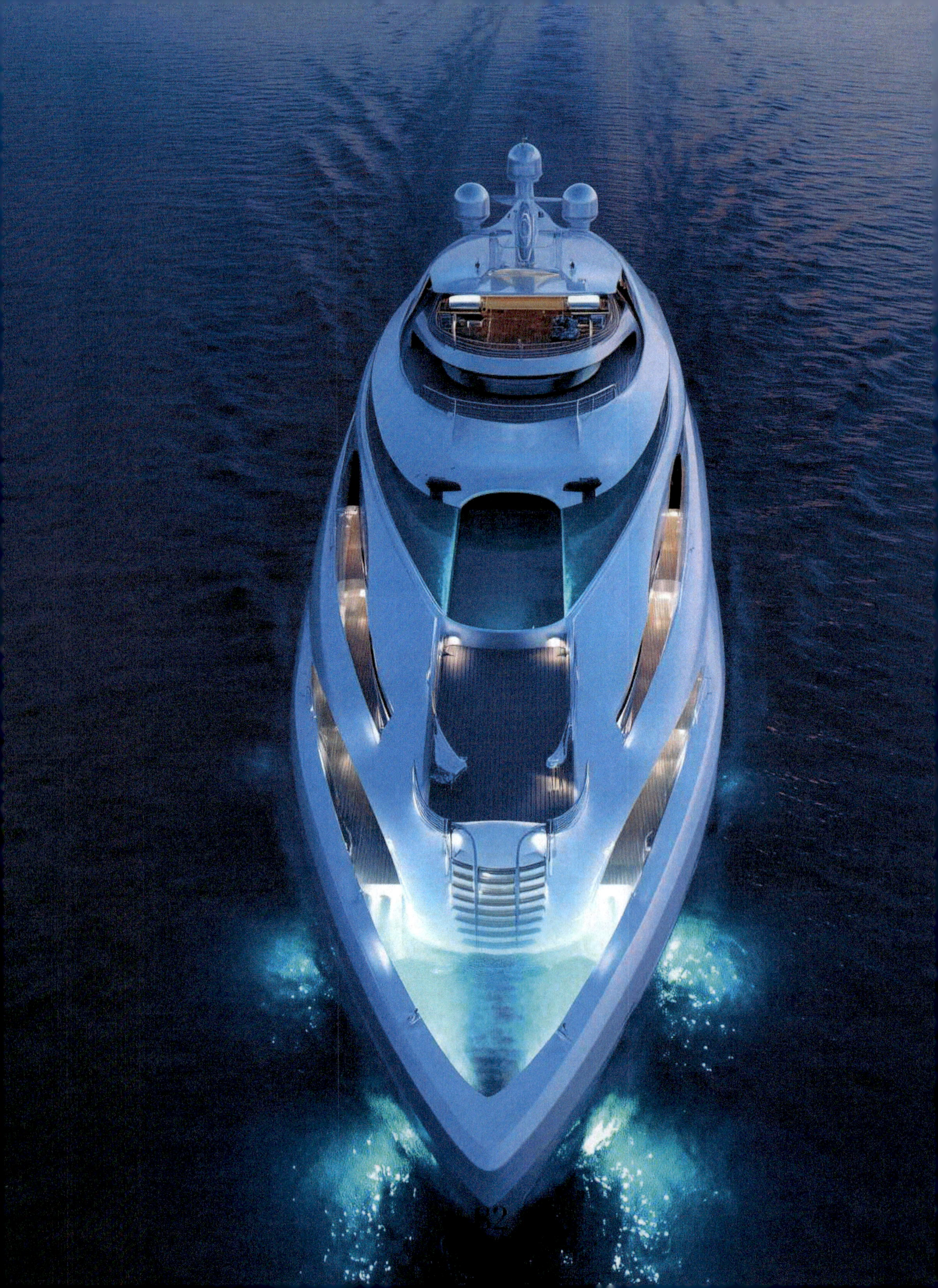

MY FAMILY IS MY HOME	I LOVE. I VALUE. I CARE.

TOGETHER WE ARE STRONG	FAMILY IS MY HEART	WE ARE A TEAM
I AM FOR THEM. THEY ARE FOR ME	FAMILY IS MY SUPPORT	I FEEL LOVED AND SUPPORTED BY MY FAMILY
I LIVE IN HARMONY WITH MY FAMILY	LOVE LIVES HERE	I CREATE TRADITIONS THAT STRENGTHEN FAMILY TIES

I AM A MONEY MAGNET	I ATTRACT WEALTH WITH EASE

I AM A MILLIONAIRE IN THE MAKING	MY INCOME IS ALWAYS GROWING	MONEY FLOWS TO ME CONSTANTLY
I WELCOME FINANCIAL MIRACLES	I OPEN NEW SOURCES OF INCOME	I LIVE IN ABUNDANCE AND STABILITY
I BELIEVE IN MY FINANCIAL LUCK	I RECEIVE MONEY WITH JOY	I AM RICH IN EVERY WAY

84

I WAS BORN TO SHINE		THE SPOTLIGHT LOVES ME
I AM SEEN. I AM CELEBRATED	MY NAME OPENS DOORS	I AM RECOGNIZED FOR MY GIFTS
FAME FLOWS TO ME EFFORTLESSLY	I INSPIRE MILLIONS	THE WORLD KNOWS MY NAME
I AM A STAR — ON AND OFF STAGE	I BELIEVE IN MYSELF AND MY ABILITIES	APPLAUSE FOLLOWS ME

MY IMAGINATION HAS NO LIMITS		I NURTURE LITTLE DREAMERS
CREATIVITY FLOWS THROUGH ME	CHILDREN INSPIRE MY SOUL	I GROW A WORLD OF WONDER
PLAY IS SACRED	MAGIC LIVES IN EVERY CHILD	I LEAD WITH LOVE AND COLOR
I AM A CREATIVE PERSON	I EASILY GENERATE NEW IDEAS	I AM CREATIVE EVERY DAY

86

I CRAVE KNOWLEDGE	EACH DAY I GROW

I AM ALWAYS LEARNING	WISDOM GUIDES ME	GROWTH IS MY PATH
I PURSUE EXCELLENCE	I EMBRACE CHALLENGES	I EXPAND MY MIND
LEARNING IS MY SUPERPOWER	I STRIVE FOR NEW KNOWLEDGE	I EXPAND MY HORIZONS EVERY DAY

I EMBODY BOSS ENERGY	I LEAD WITH PURPOSE

I AM ON MY WAY TO A PROMOTION	I AM A CEO IN ACTION	I BUILD POWERFUL EMPIRES
I SET BOLD CAREER GOALS — AND ACHIEVE THEM	I RISE. I LEAD. I WIN	I WALK WITH HIGH HEELS AND HIGHER STANDARDS
I MOVE FORWARD TOWARDS SUCCESS	I ACHIEVE MY CAREER GOALS	I OPEN NEW HORIZONS FOR MYSEL

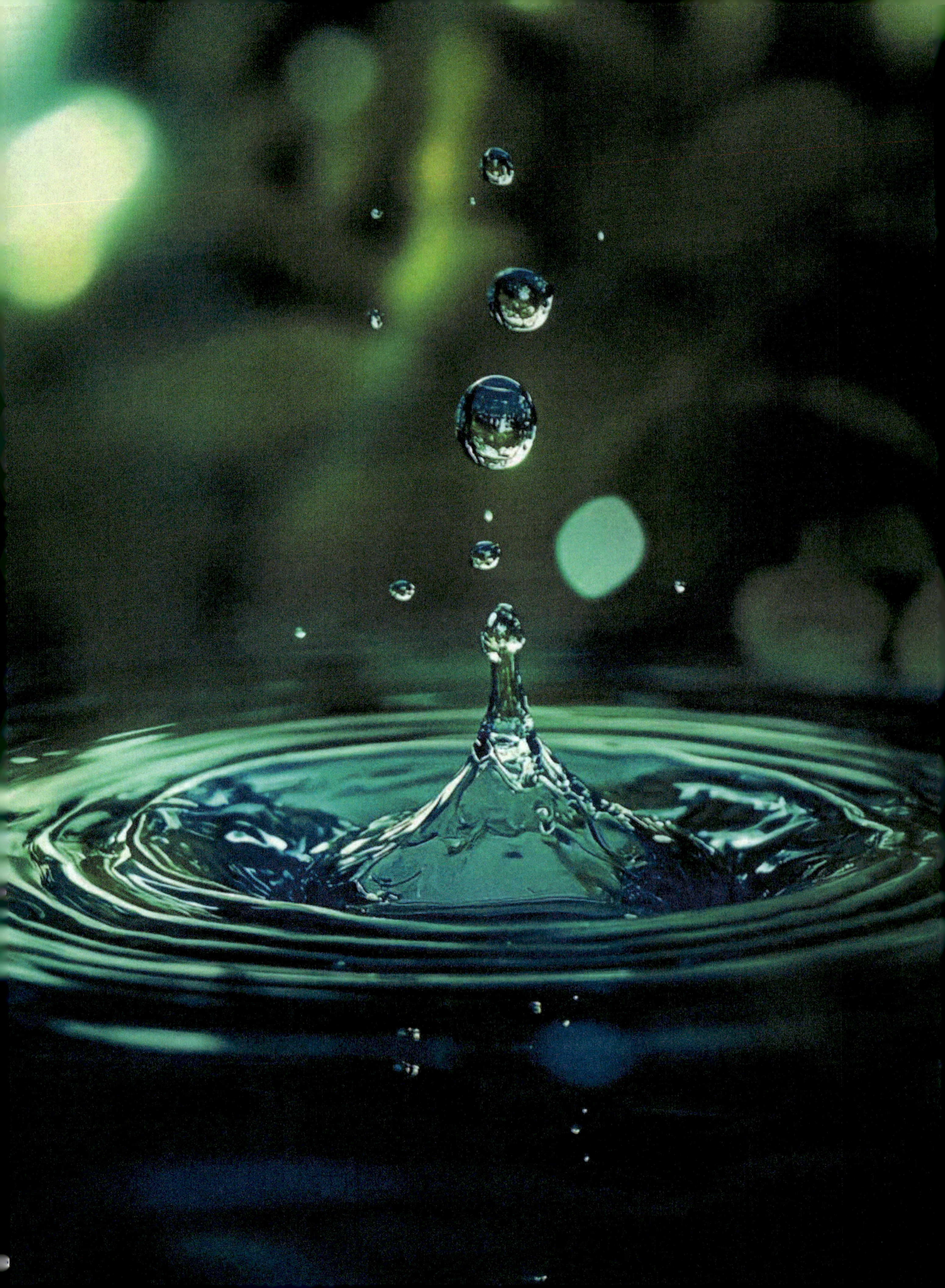

Printed in Great Britain
by Amazon